A Mermaid's Tale

A Personal Search
for Love and Lore

AMANDA ADAMS

A Mermaid's Tale

GREYSTONE BOOKS

Douglas & McIntyre Publishing Group

Vancouver/Toronto/Berkeley

Greystone Books
A division of Douglas & McIntyre Ltd.
2323 Quebec Street, Suite 201
Vancouver, British Columbia
Canada V5T 4S7
www.greystonebooks.com

Library and Archives Canada Cataloguing in Publication
Adams, Amanda, 1976–
A mermaid's tale : a personal search for love and lore / Amanda Adams.

Includes bibliographical references and index
ISBN-13: 978-1-55365-117-8 · ISBN-10: 1-55365-117-0

Editing by Nancy Flight
Copyediting by Mary Schendlinger
Jacket and text design by Jessica Sullivan and Naomi MacDougall
Jacket illustration © Stephen St John / National Geographic / Getty Images
Excerpt in Chapter 2 of "Book 12: The Cattle of the Sun" is from
The Odyssey by Homer, translated by Robert Fagles © 1996 by Robert Fagles.
Used by permission of Viking Penguin, a division of Penguin Group (USA) Inc.
Printed and bound in China by C&C Offset
Printed on acid-free paper
Distributed in the U.S. by Publishers Group West

We gratefully acknowledge the financial support of the
Canada Council for the Arts, the British Columbia Arts Council,
and the Government of Canada through the Book Publishing Industry
Development Program (BPIDP) for our publishing activities.

For Dan

And in memory of Zeki,
my little crazy-making siren

 Contents

THE MERMAID

I make my way as a mermaid,
as they wrap themselves in raincoats and plunge into
the shower,
I always go out in my golden scales on the shore.
They will say: here's the moonlit sea splash-flashing
under my tail
The thousand-eyed will see its likeness in me.

City, city you are old and you barely fill the eye
how the air congeals, like a bird and a lion
and how it strips scales from off my scaly skin,
how brave and tender I stand in the light
of the world.

And scales float onto a merchant vessel
from Thebes.
The wind is long and comely, slow in its flight.
They drift like snowflakes, like tea leaves—
my stiff attire.
They will say: Look the sea sparkles and gulls hang in the air.

TATIANA SHCHERBINA

Celadon
SEAS

Down where the mermaids

Pluck and play

On their twangling harps

In a sea-green day ...

WALTER DE LA MARE, "OFF THE GROUND"

Crimson-tailed mermaid in a celadon sea—this is how I see her. Blood-red scales that glint in clear green water. Long hair that trails past scaled hips, unfurling in waves of dark brown and black, hair that swims alongside and against the mermaid as a second living thing.

Skin burnished to a shine by the gritty texture of the sea. The salt has swirled around her shoulders for so long that they gleam like porcelain, illuminating her lissome form when seen from a distance, when spied from the boat's helm, or, when things are going badly, from beneath it. In some oceans, her shoulders are the color of chocolate, warmed by tones of orchid purple and blushed gold; in other places, her skin glows like milky carnelian stones lit from within by flame.

One sweep of her tail carries her through those thick clumps of current where the frigid northern water has thrown its fist into blankets of southern warm. The mermaid arches her back, unrestrained by a stiff spine, and raising her arms above her head, she cuts through the tangled tide like a diver through air.

Her necklace jangles like giant wind chimes when she flips over. Above the reverberating bass tones of whale mothers and the calls of sea lions, the metallic clanking of crucifix and knife, metal soup cans against crooked nails, spits a cacophony of noise into the muffled sea. Strung around her long neck is a heavy collection of offerings and bribes, gifts and garbage, all got from a century's worth of sailors. A chrome-spark necklace made of twisted bubble-gum wrappers, steel bells, broken mirrors, rosary beads, butter knives, latches, one rusty compass, and a slew of fish hooks in different shapes and sizes all hung on hand-coiled rope.

Tied into her hair are her favorite things: a small hand mirror with gilded edges and mother-of-pearl inlay; a dozen or so fat pearls, big as gumballs; a smooth piece of ivory carved into the shape of a bear and another carved into the silhouette of a gull; a pair of lacquered chopsticks, and a bottle opener in the shape of a plump tuna with a laughing mouth and the words "Fat Fish 1988" inscribed upon it. This item she picked up from an exceptionally attractive fellow paddling all alone in a kayak in foul weather. He never made it home.

This mantel's worth of trophies draped across the mermaid's chest were not the only things she had snagged. When sailors threw their nearly finished cigarettes and cigars overboard, she sometimes caught them and smoked in the sea. Standing upright on her tail, she would puff on damp tobacco, prompting stories of deep-sea chimneys, fire-breathing whales, and lost volcanoes for years to come. Wine and brandy in bottles still corked were another favorite; they brought heat to her chest and new songs—she thought her very best songs— to her lips.

This crimson-tailed mermaid had spent her day swimming around her favorite haunts: frothy coastlines that swept up towards pretty town churches and green pastures, harbors, and comfy coves with views of a village and the comings and goings of all the people in it. When she could, she waved to onlookers while bobbing seductively in the sea until the women screamed and the men ran across the sand, soaking their pant legs with sea foam. She mocked the sound of broken carriage wheels with her high-pitched, dolphinlike squeal, making crabby drivers pull over and kneel to the ground, cursing as they inspected the spokes of their wooden wheels in search of damage. General mischief making was the mermaid's delight. She charmed young girls to the water's edge with simple melodies, and when they came to her—always one by one, hesitantly—she brushed her long hair before them, singing to the sky, and flapped her tail with bravado, making the allure of mermaidenry impossible to resist.

With the young boys, she persuaded them to come near with cries for help. As she splashed her arms in the otherwise calm sea, feigning her own drowning, the boys rushed to assist with both courage and the sudden excitement of becoming heroes. When they came, she caught them by the fingertips and pinched their thumbs until they promised upon their lives, their mothers', and their pet dogs' to bring her baskets full of apples, which she loved. Come next morning, the sea's edge was lined with laundry baskets and metal pails piled high with red fruit.

Mermaids, generally, are storm makers as well as apple eaters, and when the town bell—any town bell, in any coastal village—called out the five o'clock hour, this mermaid blew, with only the strength of a mild-hearted whistle (more than that and a hurricane was born), until she had whipped up a robust gale and waves to match. Widening spirals of ruffled navy-and-white crest gathered beneath the twirling of her fingers. Laughing, she called in the clouds until they banged thunder and splintered lightning and the mermaid rode the high-lifting waves just as a child shoots down the ramp of a schoolyard slide.

Despite the inconveniences the mermaid causes—death, sore thumbs, inflated imaginations and bursting hearts, severe weather, broken marriages, and ocean storms that mangle boats and docks—she is revered as the grand dame of the sea. She is also a capricious woman of fairy-tale limb, and no one would deny that the mermaid is truth or that her tail is an enviably handsome shade of red. Too many men and women have seen that tail at dusk, when the lowering sun sets her fins ablaze and she sits smoking damp cigarettes on a rock. Although some have mistaken her for a faraway lighthouse or a poor ship on fire, many have seen, clearly enough, the rounded hips and certain face of a woman.

General mischief making was the mermaid's delight.

CELADON IS THE COLOR of pale jade or willow leaves, seen in Japanese teacups and in late June skies in northern places. It was only a few years ago, while working in a ceramics studio and glazing all my pots this very color, that I decided upon the sort of sea I would swim in: misty green. Beneath my dark blue jeans, my average legs turn to

garnet fins, and I push back from human conversation and habit to dive into the sure depths of imaginary oceans.

Every woman chooses the color of her tail, her ocean, her method of enchantment. Mermaids have never been a rare or unusual obsession. For even the cynics and the too-serious have played mermaid in the pool, whether at age six or sixty-six. Impossible not to bask in that blossoming sense that magic is at hand when one is underwater, suspended in a place that never fails to renew a certain animal bliss. Sinking to the bottom of a swimming pool, ears humming with the drone of muffled white sound, goggled eyes watching broken sun on the water's surface, who can deny experiencing a touch of "merm" when pushing off an aquamarine wall with bent legs and torpedoing through the chlorinated water in a swivel of seal grace? Legs propped up on the tub's edge evoke the tail, all curvy and oily with bath products and the sea-foam bubbles they make. Even legs swaddled in bedroom sheets and blankets can look surprisingly fishy and glamorous when viewed the right way.

The beauty of the tail is only half of the mermaid's story. Her womanly spirit—her strength and her charms—are merely complemented by the scales that wrap around her hips. It was never the fishy

‹ *Redheaded mermaids have long enchanted the green seas—and the fishermen in them.*

bit alone that drove men mad, that beckoned them to crash their ships into rocky shores and forsake all human comfort for the faraway ocean floor and dangerous waves. It was the allure of that unattainable woman who possessed, and expressed, the ocean's mystery and depth in her limbs.

Stepping back from the pool's edge, then—from sparkling crimson tails and beckoning fins—we arrive at this book's quest: Why has the mermaid legend persisted for millennia in nearly every part of the world? Why has this woman of fact or fiction never disappeared beyond the shores of our collective imagination? Why has the mermaid, quite literally, swum around the globe, netting the fascination and adoration, the fear and devotion, of people and cultures ranging from the Arctic Inuit to those who live along the coast of southern Africa? And where did her tale originate?

Various collections of Native American history and legend tell the story of a time thousands of years ago when ice sheets unfurled across the northern hemisphere like giant white carpets. All the water became solid, and the sea sucked in and sank. Continental shelves were exposed like the seams on the inside of a shirt—the earth's stitching laid out. In places, the Bering and Chukchi seas dropped to their sandy bottoms and land bridges rose out of the shallow waves.

Animals were scarce, the oceans were too frozen to fish, and the wind was too murderous to travel through; the people began to starve. Areas where green ferns once grew became nothing more than winter wastelands; summers no longer replenished the meat cache, and food became impossible to find. Desperate, the people sat close together for warmth and resigned themselves to dying.

One little girl rebelled against this impending doom. She jumped to her feet and ran outside. The cries of the others were quickly muted by the sharp winds. Frozen snow stung her cheeks like burning sand, and she pushed her way east towards the shoreline, eyes hardly open to the wind's assault.

A dark smudge on the landscape soon appeared. She drew closer to it, closer and closer, until the form became clearly human. When she finally reached the creature, she saw that it was an affable merman sitting with his tail submerged in a seal's breathing hole.

She greeted the merman and begged him for food. When he told her that he could never bring enough, day in and day out, to support her people for the length of an ice age, she asked for help. He clapped his hands and sang the sea's first chantey while pointing east and nodding his round head yes. From out of his hair he pulled the bone of a bear and a pink scallop shell, telling the little girl that she should show the elders these things as a promise and proof of food.

It took one cycle of the moon for her to convince everyone that they had to pack up and leave. During the dark of the new moon, nightmares of drowning in green light, of being trapped beneath ice, shook the group. And during the crescent moon, they feared the loss of their flint knives to the sea, the loss of hunting prowess; they lamented turning their backs on a landscape they and their ancestors had known so well. But as the moon grew wide and full and the cheeks of their children grew thin and sallow, the adults decided that they had nothing to lose by leaving—only death. The full moon was one of the largest and brightest anyone could remember. They called it hope.

They carried their boats and belongings across the ice and set them on a thin channel of swift-moving water, a small ice-free corridor between steep cliffs of pale turquoise and white. The merman sang songs to them as they began their journey east. He sang of the sand they would feel beneath their toes, of gentler winds and softer snows. His two tails would lift out of the waves like legs pedaling a bicycle, two gold-scaled arrows that people could see through fog and storm and starlight. The only time they lost sight of him was when the sun set in a blaze of gold and his fins all but evaporated in coppery light.

Mermaids, generally, are storm makers as well as apple eaters.

During the journey, no land could be seen in any direction. Even the glaciers disappeared, and the world became a seamless surface of heaven and earth, the cloudy color of the inside of a pearl. People's vision had doubled: two suns, two moons, two birds for every one seen overhead. The ocean was a mirror, and everything above was reflected below; people grew disoriented and dizzy; children buried their faces in their mothers' laps to set their eyes straight. But there was only one merman, and he kept them on their course.

When the group finally came to the end of their journey, the people pulled their boats up onto the ancient shores of today's Baja California, and that is where they made their first home in the new land.

These legends of the merfolk have temporal depth, deep as the ocean's darkest canyons. The oldest stories are not about seduction or shimmer but rather about the earliest struggles of humankind—the first groans of the earth and its inhabitants as they encountered its rugged landforms and survived its unpredictable seasons. The original merfolk were blessed with the skill of sage counsel: they shed light in the dark nooks and crannies of barely born human societies. These early stories were also part of a larger fabric of oral traditions passed on generation to generation.

The first written mer-story described a robust Babylonian mer-man who gave the first city dwellers the cuneiform alphabet. Oannes, Babylonian fish-god also known as Ea by the Greeks, rocked the cradle of civilization approximately seven thousand years ago; his likeness was described in fragments of old text and rendered on the faces of coins. Like the golden-tailed fish-man of North American indigenous belief, Oannes also took pleasure in a little humanistic rescue work here and there.

As merman king of the world's first city, Oannes was regarded as a benevolent instructor who aimed to "soften the manners of mankind." To this day he is credited with all things good and honorable in human nature: he replaced streaks of barbarism with the intelligence and somber profundity of the thoughtful sea. Rising from the waves each morning, he taught his followers how to sow seeds and nurture plants, build homes, and organize societal law. He dabbled in early mathematics, enlightening his pupils about the basic principles of geometry, and he pontificated on the virtuous nature of the arts. Famously, he encouraged his students to press reed tips into clay tablets, articulating the basic rules of inscription and the value of writing. So Oannes, the first tail to appear in writing, is also the originator of writing.

The tail's history begins to come clear: it is as old as the world's first people; it inspired and led the first human migrations from one continent to another; merfolk had a utopian vision of peace, harmony, and the pursuit of the intellect for all people of the world; they were bona fide fishy philosophers and saviors of humanity. But where are early mermaids?

Like human women, fish-tailed women were largely written out of the past and later written in only when they became temptresses and *femmes fatales*—creatures, in other words, that men were forced to succumb to or overcome. They became a lascivious backdrop to manly exploration and the source of blame for foul weather and lives taken by storm. Although mermaids were surely capable of speaking to the winds and brewing an impressive set of waves whenever or wherever they wished (we love them for this), we still have to wonder where the wise and beautiful partners of these early and chivalrous merman gods are.

> *Mermaids commonly offered their assistance to early explorers like these men in Newfoundland.*

It is known that Oannes had a wife named Damkina, Queen of Waters, and a daughter Nina, also known as Nineveh. Presumably, any wife of a fish-tailed god and Queen of Waters would be a mermaid herself. The historical record is vague about these women (and specifically their lower extremities), though one can, I think, safely assume that the altruistic fish-man would share his deep-sea abode with only the loveliest and most intelligent of mermaids. Similarly, the fish-tailed man of North America was a solitary creature for the duration of his great journey, but on the western shores of the New World he joined more of his kind, including mermaids with sumptuous hair lounging smart and porpoise-pretty on the rocks.

The ocean's first mermaids are as elusive and shadowy as the sea itself, but threads of possibility are tangled in the currents and jumbled in the pages of written history—and in the spoken verse of oral traditions—suggesting that the mermaid legend is much older than commonly thought.

Besides this temporal depth, the mermaid also has some significant geographical breadth. Few bodies of water are without their mermaid lore. Enduring temptress of the open sea, the ice-covered fjords, and muddy riverbeds, the mermaid is everywhere. Who knew that mermaids could dwell in ancient wells and freshwater streams? They sleep beneath palm trees and sit combing their tangled hair beneath hard, cracked ice. The mermaid even makes her way along city streets. In bedrooms, children fall asleep to stories of her sweet nobility and benevolence; men may well drift off to dreams of the racier sort. And women have for centuries found within the mermaid reflections of themselves, symbols of womanly power and prowess, ideals of beauty both physical and spiritual. Mermaids persist in wrapping their tails around human hearts today as much as they ever did in centuries past.

Big questions surround the mermaid—questions that have been answered in Freudian terms, fit within Jungian interpretation, and deconstructed by analytical folklorists. But somehow these approaches have always struck me as a little... dry. Interesting, perhaps, but lacking in rich and pure mermaidenly allure. Over and over again, I read a scholarly article with enthusiasm only to be left with a sinking feeling that, once again, the mermaid legend had been whittled away into children's make-believe, into base symbolism, slippery scales, and sex. Every time this happened, the ocean felt a little emptier. It was as if the world's seas had been poured through a sieve, catching all the magic and mystery in aluminum mesh. The mermaid had been snatched from her dazzling abode and set in an armchair or laid out on the psychoanalyst's couch for examination.

Where was the color, the enchantment, the out-and-out glitter of mermaidenry?

From little-kid love affairs with her unconventional princess magic to more mature infatuations with her complexity and capricious nature, I've chased the "tail" and nurtured a love for the fish-woman ever since I was old enough to open my eyes under water. When I sat down to write this book, I didn't doubt that a fish-tailed muse would spring from bright blue seas and swing open the floodgates of writerly inspiration. My search for the mermaid—for her deeper meanings in lore and imagination and her entry points into the human heart—would come together as naturally as waves and sea foam merge. In places, it has.

But here is the only snag, the only pause in a fast-pouring love song to the mermaid: it is easy to articulate what excites you about mermaids as a child, but it gets a little harder as you grow up.

Fourth-grade girls are positive that they've see mermaids offshore; they are sure they've heard them singing in lakes. Loving mermaids—like fairy princesses and teddy bears that talk—comes easily to a child, and efforts to claim a state of pure mermaidenry are expected, encouraged, adorable.

But what about loving mermaids (even, ahem, *relating* to mermaids) as a newly married, twenty-eight-year-old woman? There we get into deeper water.

Lying on a warm, sandy beach, stretching your legs out long, leaning on your bent elbows, and pointing your toes out sideways to evoke a faux fin is still sort of charming, but taken too far, and depending on the company, mature versions of mermaidenry are viewed as eccentric, weird, and to some, plain freakish.

We were supposed to outgrow mermaids once we hit the teenage years, but, contrarily, that is when I sought her out most, needed her most. I embraced the mermaid as an intrinsic—but muted—element of self-identity in high-school corridors and at keg parties on redwood forest ridges, though I also began to wrestle with skepticism towards things supernatural and intangible. Immersed in a battle between heart and head, I kept my serious contemplation of mermaid love quiet for years. It tore free only on Halloween, when the sequin tail was proudly donned, or in later years, after a couple of glasses of red wine had been sipped on the beach in the company of girlfriends and the bikinis went on (or perhaps didn't) for midnight swims. Then, standing hip-deep

The ocean's first mermaids are as elusive and shadowy as the sea itself.

in the ocean, a joy so monstrous and exhilarating, a sort of howl-at-the-moon kind of happiness would kick in. Overcoming the urge to do a permanent backflip into mermaidenry, one is left wondering why mermaids can't be (and simply aren't) incorporated into our daily lives.

For people do want to believe in something. A life without some magic is tedious, and we live in a society that increasingly eschews belief and ritual. We are the poorer for it. Driving home in a snowstorm on the I-5 in Washington state one night, I listened to an interview with a songwriter on the radio. In it she described her unapologetic faith in the "great mother." It was bold, even courageous, for her to speak of crying on tropical beaches while waiting for song lyrics to come, wrapping herself in the unseen arms of womanly support, cradling her life in devotion to a higher being, a purpose, without the slightest inhibition or self-consciousness. I couldn't help but feel a twinge of envy as I drove through black night and snow falling in cherry-blossom frenzy, hunched over the steering wheel and trying to keep to the icy road. *The beauty of wild, unfettered belief.* It's as though too much schooling, too much self-conscious behavior over the years, and too much of an aversion to New Age spirituality have left me utterly jaded on matters that float above plodding empiricism and doubt. So here I am, the greatest of skeptics, and yet when I walk around the lake by my house in late afternoon, and when the sun splinters into a thousand flecks of watery light on its surface, I cannot help but hold my breath and stare. I always half expect to see a mermaid—and always fully hope.

The love I held for mermaids as a little girl was fierce. That love has persisted, but it has also changed. This book aims to elucidate the mermaid's cultural history and her impressive resilience over time and place, but it also strives to merge a little "tail" of self-discovery into the larger narrative. It is built upon questions large and small, sturdy and delicate, for surely I am as obsessed with mermaids as any Grecian sailor ever was.

Sitting at my dark cherrywood-stained desk, given to me by a friend—a classics scholar and avid surfer who had conjugated and memorized Greek and Latin verbs on its polished surface and whose copy of Homer's *Odyssey* leaned grand and heavy against its edge—I began my quest for the mermaid. Blessed by studies of antiquity and the wine-dark sea, the desk also revealed board-wax lingering in the corners of drawers, and sand showed up whenever I moved books around. Working there was like being at the helm of some large wooden boat. Upon a sea of words and love, magic and sightings, I embarked on this search for the myths and meanings of the mermaid. Who are the world's mermaids? Where are they now? Why do women delight in silky green shirts and pearly lip balm, abalone hair clips and sequin skirts? Why has the mermaid's relevance and slippery resonance never left me? How does she continue to mature alongside me, reflecting the different stages of my life as I get older? And more to the point, why, after twenty-odd years, do I still slip into the bathtub after a rotten or perfect day, close my eyes, and call upon that crimson tail?

A Tail
IN THE TUB

A LIFE *on the ocean wave!*
A home on the rolling deep,
Where the scattered waters rave,
And the winds their revels keep . . .

EPES SARGENT, "A LIFE ON THE OCEAN WAVE"

As a child, I spared no effort to get my inner mermaid out. Once the movie *Splash* was in theaters, I became increasingly convinced that what happened to Daryl Hannah could happen to me too. One accidental spray of a lawn sprinkler, a water balloon gone awry, and there I'd be: laid out on the pavement with a mermaid tail flapping beneath my Catholic-school plaid jumper, reporters everywhere.

At the mall, I made a point of buying only blue clothes until my mother, noting the color's indisputable melancholia, nixed the habit by refusing to fund it. She said I looked sad, a look not helped by the fact that I limped everywhere in hopes of evoking the legendary Little Mermaid. I also feigned an insatiable appetite for frozen fish sticks, drew pictures of mermaid tails on binders and homework assignments, kept my fingernails glittery with silver-sparkle nail polish, fell asleep swimming beneath a full moon, and woke up in an abalone sea castle. And when my mother took me to the hair salon, I would hop into the swivel chair, remove my red knit cap, graciously accept the grape lollipop handed to me, and whisper into the hairdresser's ear, "Cut it long." I wanted mermaid hair to my knees.

Although my legs were plain and dry, I always thought I was at least *part* mermaid. From the waist down, naturally.

Sitting in the bathtub with legs covered up by sea-foam bubbles, a mirror and comb on the porcelain ledge, the waist-down scenario works well. Who can claim that there isn't a mermaid tail under those bubbles?

For me, the bathtub evokes those moments when you're in the ocean, standing in the water up to your hip bones, hair falling around your shoulders, an oyster shell in your hand. Who could doubt that you're standing on true fins? The magic of mermaidenry lies in fleeting moments of in-between: between terry-cloth towel and bath water, between sand and sea. Those exhilarating moments when you first run into the ocean and the cold water slaps up against your legs, taking your breath away. That pleasant dizzy feeling that comes with lying down on your back after a brisk swim. Or standing on a boat, leaning over the rail towards skipping surf until your hair is caught in wild wind and ocean spray and the salted air catches in your throat. When, for a brief moment, you cannot quite tell if your head is above or beneath water, if you are dreaming or awake, when the urge to dive into the wide-open mouth of the riotous and sparkling sea becomes all-consuming, and when, for a split second, you envision yourself as so much more than human.

Table salt could work me into this kind of altered state, though it required an entire canister and it stung.

Bath time: running the hot water until the room was thick with steam, I would move back and forth on bare feet along the cold tile floor, evenly pouring out cup after cup of white. I would turn up the volume on my cassette player, allowing the plangent rolling of recorded waves (a nature tape purchased with babysitting money) to float off the walls and lend drama to my dip. I would brush out my hair till it fell in flat, shiny sheets past my shoulders. Propping up my inflatable seashell pillow just right, I'd step into the bathtub and pull a wet washcloth down over my eyes.

The salt crept into tennis shoe blisters, paper cuts, peeling cuticles, and tetherball bruises. I repeated, "No pain, no gain" like a mantra, sure that I was paying a requisite and worthwhile price for my tail. Somewhere it is written that earthly mermaids must suffer.

But when the tail came—and it always did—the feeling was akin to having your lower half swaddled tight in plastic wrap. Encircling my still-narrow hips, swallowing my feet, and pressing my toes flat into scalloped fins were pearl-studded fish scales. My tail was seriously fancy, and it spilled over the side of the tub, draping elegantly with delicately webbed branches of pale blue skin stretched taut between fin tips.

Tail thus set, I would glance over my textbook under the pretense of doing homework, though inevitably I would become lost in the rhythmic brushing of my giant fins; they left faint streaks of silvery glitter on the tile floor. I imagined a young sailor boy in a red-and-white-striped T-shirt tracing my tracks of mermaid sparkle, just as a gardener finds cabbage-eating snails by their pathways of glistening thread. He would toss back his shiny black locks as a young stallion would his mane and, gasping in love and instant devotion, throw my homework to the sea, wrap me in blankets, kiss me on the cheek, and set me upon his boat.

Such were the fantasies on calm spring nights. On nights when thunder rattled the windows and trees, I would throw open the bathroom windows and fall into crashing waves, dropped into westward currents as if by helicopter. My skin would grow thicker as it acclimated to cold Pacific currents, adjusting to a chilly, aqueous existence. Between my fingers shallow webs grew, and when I held them up to the light that broke through the surface of the water, I could nearly see through them. Countless fish swooshed past my waist, and as I somersaulted and dropped deeper into the ocean, the world broke into honeycombed sheets of glass bubbles.

Yes, I was in a bathtub, but then again, not really. My heart was in the sea, my head was in the sea, and there a sound like the ancient music of the spheres, snatched from the heavens and thrust down to the valleys of the ocean floor, filled my ears and mingled with my cassette player's faux waves. It was like hearing church bells through a pile of pillows. Unlike the dry lands, where sight reigns supreme, the wet is a realm of pure acoustics: laughing humpback whales and seal mothers calling for their pups, rising and falling in time to the breathing and spitting of waves.

Such fantasies and lyrical modulation were augmented by sapphire necklaces and sea-star belts, adventures with pelicans, and hours spent lounging on smooth stones with fat seal friends and gilded mirrors—until the inevitable interruptions came: time for dinner, for bed, for feeding the cat. But surely in those mermaid moments I transcended mere legs. I was better than a princess, better than a wood nymph or mere gold-dusted fairy—I had the strength of a walrus in those skinny legs of mine. It is now as it was then: the thin line dividing flesh and scale, ordinary and extraordinary, becomes blurred and not a little ambiguous when the tub is charmed.

YOU CAN GET AWAY with interrupting the bathing rituals of an eight-year-old, but beware any needless interference with mermaids more mature. When the bathroom door is closed, it should never be opened from the outside or without clear invitation. No eye should ever peer through an open keyhole; no foot should attempt to kick through the wooden doors of privacy. There are women in the world who depend upon bath taking and the solitude it affords for maintenance of their very lives.

Melusina is by far the most illustrious of all bathing mermaids, past and present. She embodies the need for expression of the tail once a week without a hint of disturbance. Closing the bathroom door only after extracting promises of absolute sequestration, she prohibits even the gentlest of knocks. It is not that she is vain or

> *The power of the sea is woven into Melusina's scales.*

selfish, only helplessly enchanted: indulgence of the tail is both her blessing and her curse.

She is not only one woman, or one mermaid, per se. The name Melusina is familiar across European countries; it has been for centuries, though her story is varied. Occasionally she is a creature more serpentine than fishy. Some have rendered the French Melusina's lower body as a surefire snake: coils of serpentine and sinister form, sinuous and dragonish. She has been labeled "double-tailed serpent, odious and winged, horrifying and terrible." During the Middle Ages and since, however, she has been depicted in both image and word as a proper mermaid with a muscular tail, scaled to the waist, either seductive or abhorrent, depending upon the taste of the viewer. Yet whether lissome and fair or hideous and webbed, she takes her baths very seriously. She is also taken very seriously. People would swear with feverish conviction that the bathing fish-woman was never a simple product of fantasy or superstition; far too many husbands have lost their beloved wives to belittle her "tail." Too many children have called her mother to deny Melusina's legitimacy, and some persist, even today, in tracing their matrilineal ancestry to her.

When she stands on human legs, Melusina walks down long stone hallways with high ceilings, wall enclaves alight with pockets of candle flame, and into the empty bathroom, her bare feet moving across cold granite. Wrapped in raw-silk robes, she twists old faucets that

Her pretty legs were swallowed whole by a fish's flank.

groan like rusty swings and let loose twin streams of rushing water. She dashes bergamot extract and wild rose into the water, draws the curtains, and steps out of her robe, leaving it on the stone floor. Steam quickly fills the room in vaporous clouds, and as folklore tells us, Melusina transforms into a mermaid with the flick of a fin. She lets her head and hair sink beneath the sheet of scented water, which, thickly infused with enchantment, sloshes and rolls against the submerged scales of her hips with the soft clattering of bamboo wind chimes.

Legends from France, Germany, and Luxembourg all attest to Melusina's timely transformation from all-woman to serpentine mermaid. In one version, the mermaid Melusina had agreed to marry Count Siegfried, founder of Luxembourg, on one condition: that every month he grant her one day and one night of absolute privacy. Because of her stunning beauty, this simple request was granted without hesitation, and the two were married.

So it began that on the first Wednesday of the month, Melusina would retire into her chambers—a network of caverns that ran underneath the streets—and reappear with the sunrise on Thursday morning. This arrangement worked out well for the couple. As fairy tales promise, they lived a charmed and happy life together for many years.

Curiosity, however, began to blossom in the mind of Count Siegfried. What was Melusina doing alone for such a span of time? He became suspicious of her fidelity to him and bitter about the cold bed that awaited him the first week of each month. So one of those Wednesdays, the Count sought out Melusina in her subterranean chambers. When he arrived at her door, he knelt down and, holding his breath, pushed his eye against the keyhole.

His beloved wife Melusina's upper half lay upright in the bathtub, and a giant fish tail filled the rest. Her pretty legs were swallowed whole by a fish's flank, and the part he loved best was covered with repellent scales. As mermaids are commonly bestowed with a very keen sixth sense, Melusina knew instantly that her state of enchantment had been spied. Recognizing her husband's wide-open eye at the door, she jumped out of the window and into the River Alzette.

The Count never saw his wife again, but rumors of her presence in the river spread. At both dawn and dusk, people reported seeing an unusually large fish break the water's surface, leaving wide ripples in its wake. Others claimed to have seen a lovely maid swimming alone just before the morning sun peeked above the dark green hills. Some put the two together.

Elsewhere, the famous legend of Melusina is embraced not just as lore but as a veritable piece of history and heritage. In France, the colors of her tail—silvery blue and white—are the colors found on the Lusignan coat of arms (as is her very image), and even King Richard I (1157–1199) better known as Richard the Lion-Hearted, went so far as to declare himself her son. There on his royal horse sat the mixture of man and merm.

I imagine that anyone wandering through the French countryside today would have at least the chance of encountering some of Melusina's offspring, for her descendants still linger, plowing fields, tending geese, and drinking wine with their dinner. I can't help but wonder if they smell of brine. And what happens to their legs when they get wet?

The French story of the mermaid Melusina spans two generations, beginning with her mother, the Fay Pressina. While out hunting, King Elinas of Albania heard the voice of a woman singing near a fountain. This woman possessed great beauty as well as notable intelligence and wit. Recently widowed, the smitten King proposed marriage to the beautiful Fay Pressina; she laid her fairy hand upon him, saying that she would indeed become his wife so long as he never visited her during her time of lying-in.

Soon thereafter she gave birth to three daughters in one day: Melusina, Melior, and Palatina. In his tremendous excitement, the King ran down the labyrinthine halls and threw open the doors of the new mother's bedroom. The Fay Pressina was in the midst of bathing the three girls, each in turn. Held over a gleaming tub of silver, the naked girls kicked and yelped with delight, their naked feet and fists pounding the misted air and splashing the soapy water. Yet when she saw the King—a man paralyzed at the open door, filled with dread, realizing the inevitable consequence of his careless action—the Fay Pressina cried out that he had broken his word. The stupid man! What happiness destroyed! She seethed in a beaten whisper that she must now leave and, moreover, that she would take the three girls with her.

Mother and daughters went to live on the Lost Island, a place that people were rumored to find only by chance. Even if one had already been there, there was no guarantee of finding one's way back, for the island was as nebulous as the clouds wrapped around it: granite cliffs and high peaks chewed into thunderclouds, and snowdrifts blended into the cottony brumes. From a distance, one saw no land, only a massive slate of churned sky and stone, like stiff cream cast in shadow.

The girls grew up here, blessed with exceptionally pretty faces and the benefits of cold mountain air. Every morning their mother woke them at sunrise, when the land they had been forced to leave was bathed in its most flattering, rose-hued light, the city twinkling with sparks of firelight, so that they might gaze upon it and remember. It was so far away it might as well have been in a world beneath the sea.

The Fay Pressina reminded her three daughters that had it not been for their father's broken promise, had he not burst in on them when told to stay away, they might still enjoy the pleasures of the city, the company of other young people, succulent foods, and other luxuries. Melusina grew increasingly bitter. On her fifteenth birthday, she construed a plot to take revenge upon her father. She persuaded her two sisters to join her, and the three girls cast a spell on the King, stole his wealth, and left him locked in a high mountain called Brandelois.

Furious with their display of arrogance, the Fay Pressina punished them according to level of guilt. Her two sisters received only heated reprimands; Melusina, being the primary conspirator, suffered most: her mother cursed her with the tail. Every Saturday, Melusina was to become a mermaid until she met a man who would marry her with the promise of never seeing her on a Saturday. Even then, she would still have to reckon with what some might call the inconvenience of scales.

Forced to go, Melusina left the Lost Island, and after long months of wandering through the forests of France in search of the man who might redeem her, she arrived at last in the wooded glades of Colombiers. All the fairies of the trees, ponds, and lakes rushed to greet Melusina—a twinkling crowd of dragonfly wings, red lips, and blushed cheeks among dark-silhouetted tree branches and gnarled trunks—telling her that they had been waiting for her arrival. The long-awaited Melusina was not to stay with her fairy friends for long, however.

In Germany there lives a water maid with a tail the color of a speckled jawbreaker.

By the light of the moon, a man named Raymond arrived at the Fountain of Thirst. He came upon three ladies merrily twirling rivulets of spun water with their fingertips—the most enchanting of which was Melusina.

Now when Raymond arrived at the fountain, he had blood on his hands. In a recent hunting match, his boar-spear had accidentally grazed the heart of his uncle, and the man had died on the spot. Bathed in angelic serenity, awash in moonlight, Melusina soothed his grief. She stroked his hair and brought his weeping head to her breast. Through powers of the supernatural sort, she concealed from the world the unfortunate deed he had done, and Raymond—limp in her arms and drunk with affection—asked the lovely girl to marry him. After he promised on oath never, under any condition, to seek her out on a Saturday, she agreed, and the two exchanged vows right there.

Their union was blessed with wealth, if not pure happiness. Melusina built her new husband the castle of Lusignan; she also created La Rochelle, Cloître Malliers, and Mersent. His monumental homes were spread across the French landscape. Within these stately homes, however, misfortune struck, for Melusina gave birth to a motley crew of deformed creatures, including one with a boar's tusk projecting from its mouth. But despite her mysterious absences and the growing family of monsters, Raymond's love for the woman who had ravished both his heart and his eyes remained steadfast.

Fate, however, was determined to shape things otherwise. One day, Raymond's cousin appeared at the house, and over glass upon glass of dandelion wine, he led Raymond to doubt and worry, poking holes in the poor man's unconditional spousal faith. He led Raymond to believe that Melusina spent her Saturday afternoons in the arms of another lover. So the very next Saturday, Raymond hid himself in Melusina's supposed trysting place—her bathing quarters.

When she had settled in the tub, it was not quite horror that seized him at the sight of her gray, sky-blue, and white scales, but rather deep-cutting anguish. Through his breach of faith, he knew that he had risked losing his wife forever. He remained hidden beneath curtains as she soaked, each flop of her tail a fist to his belly, each song from her lips a rain of splinters upon his broken heart. Setting himself

‹ *Even men in tights have found mermaid love at the water's edge.*

against fate, Raymond remained silent; he would never reveal to a soul what he had witnessed. At least this was the plan.

He remained silent until the day calamity struck his household. His two monstrous sons had been carelessly lighting the hunting torches, and the window curtains caught fire. Flames engulfed the room, and the boys turned against each other, crazed by the pain of blistering burns. Each blamed the other for the destruction of their father's home, and the hallways erupted with the sound of hot anger and insults. Raymond left the scene, slammed the door of his bedroom, and buried his head in his hands, incensed at the perpetual drama of his strange, dysfunctional family. Melusina opened the door and ran towards him—ready to offer comfort and condolence for the unfortunate fire—but, being too angry to think, Raymond seethed, "Out of my sight, thou pernicious snake and odious serpent! Thou contaminator of my race!" Melusina drew back in grief and horror. Three steps back and she fainted. When she finally revived in the arms of her distressed husband, she told him that she must now depart:

> But one thing I will say unto thee before I part, that thou, and those who for more than a hundred years shall succeed thee, shall know that whenever I am seen to hover over the fair castle of Lusignan, then will it be certain that in the very year the castle will get a new lord; and though people may not perceive me in the air, yet they will see me by the Fountain of Thirst; and thus shall it be

so long as the castle stand in honor and flourishing—especially on the Friday before the lord of the castle shall die.

She did not take the children with her, as her mother had done with her as a babe, but she continued to tend to them. It was rumored among the house staff and local townspeople that at night a shimmering figure would approach the cradles and that the little ones held out their arms in welcome. She would suckle the children, set them upon her blue-and-white hip for a lullaby, and disappear at dawn.

Thereafter, Melusina became visible only when death was about to claim one of her own. Some claim that she lives as a specter of the night, shrieking and flying on pointed wings about the castle, circling the stone towers in writhing agony and despair. The lamentations of her family following her departure were rumored to be so loud and Melusina's wailing so desperate that the phrase *le cri de Mélusine* is used even today in France to describe the distressed cries of hunted animals.

In some of Melusina's manifestations, her tail is more candy sweet than reptilian. In Germany there lives a water maid with a tail the color of a speckled jawbreaker—rainbow flecks sprinkled on lacquer-white scales. Her story begins with a lost knight.

Disoriented after the fast chase of a wild boar, the knight was lost and left wandering aimlessly through the woods. He set his course into the lowering sun, walking in wide circles. He was always sure that the southern horizon and its receding tree line were close, but then he always found himself at the point he had reached before. The forest had become a canopy of confusion, an indistinct jumble of undergrowth and thick-bark tree trunks that all looked exactly the same.

Singing to himself, tripping on fallen wood, grabbing at the branches of large bushes and tall-stalked plants as if they were out-stretched hands, the knight was in bad shape when he stumbled upon a high-walled castle, surrounded by water, in a large meadow. The drawbridge was suspended, and though he called out and whistled and waited, no one came to greet him, and not a sound was heard. He decided to wait.

By the time it grew dark, however, his patience had nearly expired. He figured that the forest offered better company than a lone castle and picked up his things to go. He did not need the sealed doors of humanity and unattainable kitchens staring him in the face, mak-ing a mockery of his predicament. But it was then, as he turned to walk away, that he saw a girl emerge from the trees. Her hips moved like full water buckets, heavy and slow, reminiscent of that ingredi-ent most tempting to a lost man's dry mouth. He thought to himself, "Wait! She knows her way around here. She is going inside."

He asked the girl if she might ask permission for him to enter. She, being owner of the fortress, told him that that was unnecessary and that if he liked, he could come with her. She stepped upon a hidden stone and the bridge lowered. With a large key she unlocked the front gate, and they walked together through a courtyard filled with bright fruits and birds—birds he had not heard outside the high walls—each of gem color and music-box sound. The girl led the knight into a stately room furnished in rich wood and brass fixtures and told him to make himself comfortable. She said that she would make a meal, for she was hungry and no doubt so was he. She had no servants and would see to the meal herself.

The best elements

Within the snap of two fingers, she re-turned with a fine roast, cakes, wine. The two talked long into the evening, and soon the knight felt sorry for the girl who lived alone in the big castle. He asked if time passed slowly for her, but she said no, only that sometimes she wished for company and conversation.

of mermaidenry

are tucked beneath the

scales of privacy.

The knight needed no more of an invitation. He suggested that he might stay for a few days, and the girl said she would be happy with that. Of course, one day became three, three became a week, one week became a month, and so on. They became so accustomed to one another that the knight eventually asked if she would like to be his wife. The girl gave ready consent, so long as he promised to let her have Fridays to herself and not to follow her. They settled into an easy life of husband and wife. Lovely children were born, and their happiness lacked nothing.

Such joy is bound for interruption, and it arrived with the rattle and bang of stones against the front gate from the dirty fist of a second lost knight. The relentless heaving of rocks caused the husband to open the castle doors. Certainly he remembered the harshness of being lost in the forest and the hunger it brought.

They sat at the table, and the strange knight inquired about the lady of the house, as she had not yet made an appearance. Her husband explained that his wife was never seen on Fridays, and in keeping with his promise, he never sought her out. "What kind of housewife would not tell her husband where she could be found?" the strange knight demanded to know. "Nothing good could come of such behavior."

This conversation so alarmed the husband that he set out to find his wife. He searched everywhere: beneath the courtyard trees that were always in bloom no matter the season, in the children's rooms, along his wife's favorite strolling paths. At last he came to the cellar, where he found a door. He paused and he sighed, he stepped back, but then stopped. His mind was flooded with indignation and in a snap of jealousy and fear, he flung open the door. There, swimming in a small pond, was his mermaid wife—who, when she met his eyes, cast a somber glance at him and then disappeared.

He ran back upstairs to tell the strange knight of his experience, but the man had also disappeared. The husband and his faithful wife had been cruelly deceived. The husband grieved so hard for his lost wife that his heart finally split in two, and one by one the lovely children died. The castle fell into ruins, and as they say today, it is not even known where it formerly stood. Only the tale remains.

INTERFERENCE WITH THE TAIL is an inevitable deal-breaker. As Melusina shows, the tail in the tub is analogous to the dark beauties of a secret. The best elements of mermaidenry—the secrets, the peculiar beauty, the otherworldliness of the sea—are tucked beneath the scales of privacy, hidden from the world, and indulged in only when alone and unwatched.

As a little girl, I guarded my mermaid secret, leaning upon it as if it were some supernatural crutch, some trick up my sleeve that I had ready to reveal to the world, if I chose. The shame of being picked last for a kickball team, of not being invited to a birthday party—so serious and upsetting at the time—was washed away by dreams of mermaidenry. Although you might never disclose the tail, it always offered solace. A sort of *fall at my fins* potential. The tail was the ticket out of the expected and ordinary.

The bathtub is not just a place where the tail flies free, stretched out in fish-scaled glamour, but it is also, perhaps more importantly, a privately kept secret—like a page torn from a diary, folded, and locked away in box. Above redemption, enchantment, desire, and cursed fate, the stories of Melusina suggest that a happy marriage must be fully consummated not only in the couple's bed but also in the bath. Melusina's request for uninterrupted time to herself is a form of self-preservation in an otherwise complete union.

Not many secrets are kept in good marriages, or so convention holds. We reveal our most intimate selves to the spouse, to the kindred soul. All is illuminated, no corners left in shadow. Or are good secrets sometimes kept? Is that perhaps what keeps attraction alive? By demanding crystalline faith from her partner, Melusina makes clear that although she is willing to share her life with another, certain things shall remain entirely her own. She keeps a piece of herself for herself.

Some interpretations of the Melusina myth argue that the bathing mermaid is involuntarily tossed between states of power and powerlessness, that her tail symbolizes not a fierce show of earthly liberation and personal autonomy but rather vulnerability. For while in a state of enchanted "merm," she is at risk of losing all she loves: husband, children, home. But one has only to consider the punishment dealt to the trespassing spouse and the fact that she abandons her home of her own accord, even if in sorrow, to recognize that Melusina's power as a mermaid lies in her decision to act in accordance with her own priorities. She might just love the tail a little more than the rest.

For the tail can never be possessed by another. It is entirely hers—be it blessing or curse—and thus it cannot be changed, diluted, or ignored by anyone else. Possessing such an untouchable form of selfhood lends confidence to one's gait, bestows on one a pride in the ability to surprise, even shock, to remain a bit unknowable. And what could startle more than turning to one's lover over dinner—perhaps a typical Wednesday night meal of pork chops and potatoes—and saying, "Dear? I am a mermaid, always have been. Here, let me show you." Surely a mermaid's tail is a treasure best not shown or explained to another. For who would understand or value it as you do?

Misunderstanding could prove unbearable: imagine someone shrieking in horror at a thing you loved and cherished above all else, despising what you thought most beautiful. No wonder Melusina sprouted wings in her rage and flew out the window.

As her tail illustrates, then, good marriages—or any relationship, for that matter—"lack nothing in happiness" when unmitigated respect is granted to one another. Lovely children may be born, ease and contentment bless the couple's life; all is indeed a fairy tale made true, *until* one craves possession over another person's independence—when suspicion translates into jealously and vice versa. That dart of insecurity and fear, that creeping feeling of threat, of being made a fool of, is what deals the deathblow to the once sturdy relationship. "Desire makes everything blossom," mused the French novelist Marcel Proust. "Possession makes everything wither and fade."

Running in search of his wife, blinded by anger and unwarranted trepidation, the husband bursts in on his bathing lover and, in doing so, betrays her greatest and only wish: to be left alone. Her tail grows stronger, although the love she holds for her spouse begins to wither. Having suffered such disrespect towards her innermost secret and most clandestine delight, the mermaid becomes callous and firm in her resolve to depart. In sorrow or rage, she vanishes into mists or waves, never to be seen again. The husband's crime of encroaching upon his wife's private life is harshly punished, perhaps too much so.

But then, who doesn't protect her mermaid secrets?

Siren's SONG

Once Mermaids mocked your ships
With wet and scarlet lips
And fish-dark difficult hips . . .

KENNETH SLESSOR, "THE ATLAS"

Twelve years old, standing in the wet sand of a northern California beach under a blanket of fog and beneath rolling hills— of which you could see only the bottoms—I was entranced by the sirens' call. Blending their song with the melancholy bass of the local foghorn carried west in the summer winds, the sirens sang to me, *Join us, join us. Oh Mandy, step in! The cold water grows warm and the tide strokes your hair! Your tail, like ours... Fishy and fair!* I could hear this within the acoustical belly of the horn, in the pockets of breezes, in the banter of seagulls overhead.

Without further ado, I would walk to the waves. Quickly unbuttoning my blue jeans and hopping around to kick them off, my sweater with the big brown buttons thrown to the wet sand, T-shirt to the waves, I'd yank away socks and headband, sneakers and windbreaker, to stand proud in my rainbow-striped one-piece swimsuit. Some might steer boats in the direction of the sirens' songs; I would simply dive in. Raising my arms above my head and touching them at the wrists to make a sleek and perfect V-form, I arched forward, leaning into the black and white water, thick with dark, churning volcanic sand. Although I looked like a girl feigning a dive, I was quite prepared to jump, throwing human life and limb to the wind.

Join us, Oh join us! The sirens pitched higher.

Never mind the strong undertow, rip currents, hypothermia-inducing temperatures, and big waves; no, danger mattered very little. For in my thinking, once the waves had swallowed me and pushed me under with their salty and muscular licks, and I had ceased to struggle as salt water filled my lungs, I would become a silvery, white-shouldered mermaid. *Fishy and fair!* All would grow warm, and the deep-water realms would reveal themselves to be a soft and gentle place cast in an amethyst hue and verdant effulgence.

Oh Mandy, come in . . . Mermaidenry is yours if only you'll swim!

Unlike the tepid public swimming pool, this strip of beach set my mermaidenry free. I stood braced for the moment when my knees would buckle and my calves would start to feel like two slim bags of wet sand. With fists clenched and cheeks puffed out just a bit, I held my breath. I always held my breath. I waited to fall backward as my legs grew incapable of holding me upright, my stomach would flex as I folded in two, and at last I would end up lying on my back in the sand, propped up on my elbows in a brazenly dramatic calendar-girl pose. My hair would come undone and hang wild down my back, and the waves would wash over my body and face. With each rolling surge of sea foam and tide, my mermaid tail would grow brighter and stronger. It started as crumpled skin and grew luminescent and slick.

Shameless drama it was.

Eyes squeezed tight, teeth chattering, and feet still dug into the sand to hold my balance in the swirling water, ignoring the late-afternoon dimming of light and the calls from my mother, for it was "time to go home!" I swam in the ocean as a mermaid, finding a siren's embrace in each wave.

I could always feel my mermaidenry best when what should have been a fish tail—my legs and feet—were immersed in real salt water and my nose stung with the scent of pungent brine and wet seaweed. Nothing could replicate the feeling that came with cold tides pooling around my ankles and the dark beauty of knowing that the continental shelf fell steep and sharp only a few yards ahead. The depths of mermaidenly possibility, like the sirens themselves, called sweet and loud.

MY URGE TO LEAVE all behind and meld with the song of the sirens had precedent. Although I spent much of my early double-digit years in a state of near drowning, I didn't know if it was the allure of their voices alone that sank hooks into my heart or if it was the possibility of actually seeing the singing enchantresses. A cliff's jump into pretty sound or a watery dive into the girls' club at the bottom of the sea—I couldn't decide. But the longing the sirens cultivated was both fierce and steady. I was absolutely certain that one could run headlong into their song and escape unharmed. Perhaps swim into better things. How many times did we drive by the crashing waves in the family car, en route to a picnic or a day of bicycle riding in the Marin County hills, and I'd have to plead with my parents to turn the radio up, up, up, to drown out the voices I couldn't resist—the ones that poured out of the waves like waterfalls surging past tight stones. And with grown men on boats, the stakes were even higher—as was the pitch of the song.

There has always been a delicious tension between sailors and salty temptresses; the theme is most strongly anchored in the *Odyssey*. We know how it goes: the sirens and their irresistible songs are flung out over the wine-dark sea, into the hearts of men, and pressed against wax-filled ears. Singing ravishing melodies to hapless sailors passing by, the sirens of old lured spellbound mariners to their graveyard shores, turning men into piles of bones, for

> . . . Whoever draws too close,
>
> off guard, and catches the Sirens' voices in the air—
>
> no sailing home for him, no wife rising to meet him,
>
> no happy children beaming up at their father's face.
>
> The high, thrilling song of the Sirens will transfix him,
>
> lolling there in the meadow, round them heaps of corpses,
>
> rotting away, rags of skin shriveling on their bones . . .
>
> Race straight past the coast!

But few ever raced. Most lingered; many never even left. The sirens' songs were as lethal as shark attacks and more wont to happen. Requiring no provocation, the sirens of old sought out their human prey in a malicious manner. They excited the heart only to ravish and murder the body in cold blood . . . or so the old men have said.

When it comes to women of the sea, things tend to be a little more complicated than simple stories ever suggest. But all good tales require a little reading between the waves.

To begin, Homer's sirens were not fish-tailed. They were bird-women: winged and buxom with talons replacing feet and feathers standing in for flesh. Paintings on ancient ceramic pots depict handsome women with highbrow chignons in their hair and musical instruments in hand, soaring above the mast of Odysseus's ship. From their hips drop long eagle tails, etched in black and tarnished gold. In some, their arms are drawn back into large wings, and their lips are parted in song. During the tenth century, encyclopedias of the world's creatures—real and mythological, with little distinction between the two—described the sirens as women who were sparrows from the chest up: long human legs topped by the breasts and beaks of small birds. In other cases, it is the reverse: the sirens were defined as dainty birds with the faces of women. In either case, fish tails were nowhere to be found, but birdlike voices were the centerpiece of their malevolent charms.

Some say there were originally three sirens; some say five. They've been known by the following names: Thelxiepia, Molpe, Aglaope, Pisinoe, Ligeia, Leucosia, Raidne, and Teles, and there is a range

‹ *The song of the sirens—first considered*
bird-women and later given fish
tails—is cast out over the sea.

of different spellings for each, depending on the language and the preferences of the storyteller. Their island of enchantment has only one name, however: Sirenum scopuli. It was from there that all their songs came, drifting along the craggy cliffs and shorelines—poison-tipped or, more apt, *poison-lipped* song.

That song has remained a constant, an integral part of the sea's beauties and dangers, the essence of its stormy thrill; yet the appearance of the singer has changed. There was at some point a transformation from feather to fin. No one is quite certain when it occurred or why. Some speculate that it was a case of confused nomenclature. *Wing* and *fin* are the same word in ancient Greek; in Latin, only one vowel separates *pennis* and *pinnis*. Hence, the sirens' acquisition of scales may have been nothing more than the slip of some scribe's quill during the translation of an ancient text. But mistakes that good are hard to believe, and any artist would insist that women of the sea are most compelling when set upon sinuous tails; stiff feathers could only be exchanged for sensual scales. Sirens belong in the wet sea, not flying overhead.

There has always been a delicious tension between sailors and salty temptresses.

Before they laid down their wings forever, transitional sirens of both feather and fin—women with shoulder-blade wings and fish-scaled thighs—surfaced for a time, oddly enough, on tombstones. They were placed in cemeteries to guard the dead from evil spirits and to carry the deceased to eternal rest, or perhaps to an eternal good time. Over time they morphed into mourners, heads and hair lowered in graveyard grief. They stood guard over the dead in a perpetual posture of anguish and resolve, filling in for the angels and saints of today. By the eighth or ninth century CE, however, the wings had dropped, the talons were permanently retracted, and our familiar mermaid swam out of the cemetery and back to the sea. No matter what the cause of her creation, or confusion, the word *siren* had become virtually, and permanently, synonymous with *mermaid* in the Western world.

MANY HAVE INSISTED that the siren's song is only the murmur of waves in hollow caves or the whistling of wind through coastal trees, the creaking and groaning of the ship's mast in a rainstorm. They say that her melodies are the snapping of wooden planks and the slapping of sails, the mingling of gulls and salty-sea delirium, that months at sea caused the very waves to speak as they lost their bass-deep roar and pounding to become birdlike melodies light as sea foam. As I've heard it, the siren's song lies somewhere within the reedy notes of the oboe, the ringing of a fingertip circling wet crystal, and a canary's bright whistle sweeping up inside a conch shell and giving it airy, almost husky, reverberation. And the song famously builds in intensity like gray storm clouds overhead—hurricanes given voice.

Whatever it was, their songs unraveled all manly composure. They dissolved all restraint and drove men willingly to their deaths as they led their ships straight into rocky shores. How could pretty songs alone wreak such havoc? Opera audiences don't feel an urge to leap off balconies when an aria fills the theater; concertgoers survive even the best performances.

Although the melodies were definitely seductive, it was perhaps the lyrics that made men mad. *What* the sirens sang was as important as how they sang it. Tuning their song to the chord of each man's heart, the sirens tapped the innermost longings of men at sea and beckoned them near with promises of personal fulfillment. They promised Odysseus not only an answer to lustful passions but wisdom and knowledge. Sending their voices out across the air, they proclaimed that

> Never has any sailor passed our shores in his black craft until he has heard the honeyed voices pouring from our lips, and once he hears to his heart's content sails on, a wiser man.

If only Odysseus would pay them heed, boundless knowledge would be his for the taking: he would become a wiser man. Quite probably, it was this lust for things cerebral—not physical—that caused Odysseus to plead with his crew to lash his limbs tighter to the ship's mast, for his heart "throbbed to listen longer."

The words they sang: the piercing recognition that someone sees the quietest wish of your soul and articulates it to the tune of strong winds. One would feel not only seduced but, more important, known, seen, understood. As though the ivy tangles of the heart had been exposed suddenly to a window of light. Surely many sailors were forced by circumstance to be at sea for months at a time, sleeping alone in small, uncomfortable beds, craving the warmth of a woman's body, pining with lust for it, but for the softness and security of it too. They must have hoped that the haunting melodies cast over the sea issued from the fair lips of one singing straight to them, only for them. Emerging from the waves, a woman from the sea foam, long hair spread over her unclothed torso and hips, beckoning with desire to match a sailor's own.

But there are others who heard within the sirens' calls assurances of power and wealth, of shorelines littered not with the bones of their brethren but with treasure and piles of gold for the taking. Some ears heard the voices of loved ones from back home: the beautified voices of their wives, sisters, and daughters promising them a swift return home if only they'd come a bit closer to Sirenum scopuli. Lust indeed, but then also knowledge, love, fame and fortune, respite from the harrowing sea, prophecies, wisdom, eternal life or blissful death: what made the sirens' songs spellbinding was that no two were the same. Each found its target and followed its cadence of unexpressed longing. But not only sailors, and certainly not only men, fall prey to the siren's call.

FISH-TAILED SIRENS have never stopped singing. Their songs have formed the soundtrack to my life. Her seducing song always shot through me like a sweetened dart. I never knew when it would come, but it hummed in the background at all times and sometimes poured out of the radio unexpectedly and flooded my ears. The whole world would feel right again now that the mermaids were singing once more, even if I heard them while driving on a city highway or through the earphones of my Walkman.

Barely fifteen years old and by myself, rainbow-striped swimsuit fully outgrown and replaced by a tacky black Body Glove bikini with hot pink stitching up the sides and a way too high French-cut, I was home from school. I grabbed a soda and slumped on the taupe-carpeted stairs. Leaning against the oak beam that rose from stair-well to ceiling, I was pinned beneath the weight of teenage angst and new heartache. The night before I had had my first "deep" conversa-tion with my soon-to-be-ex-boyfriend, Fig, on the telephone.

I had torn giddily through the past six months, beside myself with excitement to be riding shotgun in a turquoise truck that my boy-friend actually owned. Fig lived with his sister in a hippie shack on a hill (no parents there). A place filled with spontaneous jam sessions and beer in green bottles, quartz crystal amulets, tie-dyed wall hang-ings, and tofu with brown rice swimming in organic tahini paste, food that I would have rejected had my mother served it to me, but off Fig's wooden spoon, it was amazing and I loved it.

My first serious boyfriend—I was awed by the whole scene: the brand-new kissing and commensurate heart quickening, the parties,

> *Mermaids are rarely, if ever, modest,*
> *and they are not necessarily deep.*

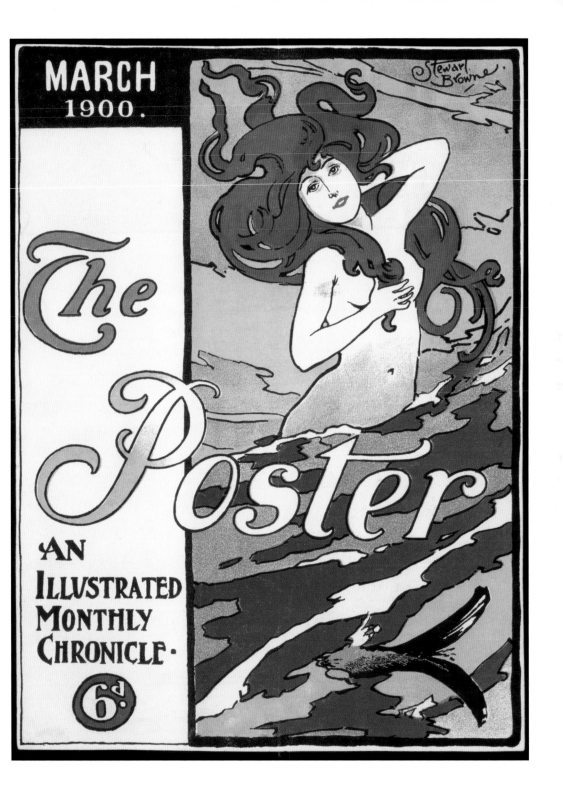

the mature crowd (five to ten years older than I). The doors of adventure were wide open. I wanted to keep this relationship going, wanted to keep riding in the blue truck with the music playing loud and Fig watching my hair blow out the window in shampooed ribbons.

Fig had mermaid hair himself: raven black and down to his waist. During evening hikes up to the fire tower behind his house, I felt the first inkling of desire to write about love. Hearing him play on his banjo, I wanted to learn flute, or at least tambourine. I started inscribing Led Zepplin lyrics into wet pottery during ceramics class. I became a vegetarian. I hung a yellow sun effigy over my bed. I became fascinated with fairies, guitar amps, and hemp while wearing patchouli oil, beaded necklaces, and flea-market tank tops with purple embroidered flowers looping around crocheted necklines. I expected that Fig and I would someday drive a Volkswagen bus into a pink California sunset. Once there, immersed in a flamingo-feather glow, we would live as generally groovy people who sought out life's deeper meanings in sandy affection and drum circles.

The phone call that left me sitting wistful on the stairs arrived after an awkward month where we, as Fig explained, "weren't connecting."

> ‹ *Although much of their lives is a blissful affair, mermaids have encountered a little heartache on the surface of the sea.*

"Don't you ever get, like, deep?" he asked. "Sorta think about stuff?" He cleared his throat.

"Yeah, I'm deep." What I was, was nervous.

Sigh. Silence. Bigger sigh that made me think of dragon nostrils. "Like, what's deep for you?"

"I don't... I don't know. Just, you know, deep." Badly stuttering and desperately trying to find a deep topic, "Deep..."

Mmm.

Silence.

What happened next was this: Fig began a long and impassioned discussion of UFOS. Aliens in space, aliens as ancestors, aliens hidden by the government in secret plastic bubbles roosted on remote mountaintops. Did I know about planet Dogstar, and just what did I think about UFOS, exactly? His dishing of deep was met by my befuddled silence.

By the time we hung up, he had broken up with me. In his words, "I think I just need to be with more of a woman who is deep." I had been ditched for my lack of depth, and I was devastated. A teenage-sized identity crisis ensued. It came fast and hard; an avalanche that I had until then succeeded in keeping at bay pummeled me to the carpeted floor. Whatever confidence I had since mustered in the delicate high-school years was bound up in being Fig's girlfriend. Without that, I was lost at sea—an intimidating, every-seat-taken, high-school-cafeteria-shaped sea.

I was painfully quiet in high-school corridors and waited out the lunch period in the photo-lab darkroom printing pictures of seascapes and shells. I didn't relate to anyone, felt strange and uncomfortable in my own skin, eschewed all extracurricular activities, and liked reading *The Unbearable Lightness of Being* but found English class unbearable. I fit in nowhere and passed up rides home offered by friends so that I could take long walks and think.

All good tales require

Emotionally lopsided and eager to please, I was at that vulnerable age at which your hips grow wide and your center is impossible to locate. A stampeding bull, a

a little reading

between the waves.

kitten, a flopping goldfish hankering for its tank: I was all of these things standing self-consciously in a pair of white leather, intentionally scrunched, past-the-ankle boots and old Levis.

Cracking open my can of diet soda (the calorie had been discovered, and we girls were all quick to call it foe), I turned MTV on with the remote control. I think I heard the piano before I saw the redheaded siren.

She divulged silvery to me, *But what if I'm a mermaid in these jeans of his* . . . Tori Amos, crouching—almost folded—into a wooden box for her music video debut, managed to cut through every layer of girl and gut to strike my core's chord.

> But what if I'm a mermaid
> In these jeans of his with her name still on it

A tidal wave of blossoming remembrance, a reconnection with my own mermaidenly worth. It was the *what if* that grabbed my heart,

that caught my ear over stormy seas. Fig sank into a watery hole, and I started swimming a stronger stroke.

When the siren's song came in clear, things changed. And some songs were clearer than others. There had been times in my life when the volume went all the way down. When the mermaid was forced into the far back of my mind for whatever reasons: embarrassment, a lack of sparkle, shaping myself to fit other people's needs instead of my own. There she sat, snugly hibernating in the darkness of my head, pressed into the farthest corners of my heart.

This still happens. How can the sirens seduce a person scrambled with racing hormones and self-consciousness? A woman too busy with career and stress and socializing? Maybe the siren's song is like the voice inside—the gut feeling that, if listened to, brings clarity and a grounded kind of knowing. Sometimes things just reveal themselves. Sometimes the sirens sing to you, saying precisely what you longed to hear: what if?

What if I'm a mermaid in these jeans . . . Every sadness and uncertainty passed. Inklings of womanly anger filled their place. I was electrified. Tori's voice merged in perfect resonance with the call of those beach mermaids I had heard so many years ago. Once more

‹ *The siren's song is often heard in the most unexpected places.*

my heart surged, just as it had when I stood in white swirling currents waiting—earnest and believing—for my tail to come. From a child's mermaid fantasies to womanly and empowering identification, I discovered—like thousands of women had before me—the potent allure of the mermaid. The clouds parted, revealing a new version of old love.

They dissolved all restraint and drove men willingly to their deaths as they led their ships straight into rocky shores.

Reconnected with my mermaidenry, then, I began walking through my teenage years with a more confident curl and strut, the kind only the tail can give. It still seems to me now that during the four minutes of that pop song, I forged a new identity, one that included a vegetable-green mermaid tail glazed with, oh, pewter and highlighted with flecks of raw umber, hidden beneath acid-washed denim. *What if* became the musical leitmotif of my teenage years, a siren's song that caressed my ear just as it had for Odysseus on that boat so long ago.

Why not be a teenage mermaid? Why not steer one's boat into song and fog? I would dream of loping down high-school corridors, smiling to my left, smiling to my right; I'd walk out for swim practice on a hot September afternoon, take off my jeans and white peasant blouse, and stun the student body with my killer curvy figure, firm as a dolphin (remember: dream). Fig would pound his fists and sob into the shoulders of his buddies. As I dove into the turquoise pool, my body oiled and shining, every pair of eyes would follow my sleek entrance into the water and the tiny splash I'd leave behind. Never mind blackout lunches in the photo lab, I would now lounge on my beach towel, much to the pleasure of the boys, and their interest in me would feel like warm sheets of sunshine lying heavy on my belly and shoulders, wrapped up in my hair. The siren's song had found me again, and the lyrics had changed. *Fishy and fair!* was no longer quite enough. The tune now ran more along the lines of *Deep-sea popularity and a tail beneath the jeans is just fine for me* . . . Sans Fig, confused and fifteen, ambivalent about everything, I had nevertheless received a tail upgrade.

THERE IS ONE MATTER left unresolved: were the sirens as cruel and bitter as described? Were they bloodthirsty? I felt only love from them, assistance, inspiration. Does temptation lead only to a bad end? Is there not a sailor who lived happily ever after with his siren? The two living their lives together, always locked in an enchanted embrace?

Don't believe in the tales invented about us; we kill none, we only love. Such were the words of siren Ligeia in Giuseppe Tomasi di Lampedusa's story "The Professor and the Siren" (1957). In it, a young man living alone for a summer on a deserted strip of Italian coastline describes what happened when a woman

with astounding vigor emerged straight from the sea as far as the waist and put her arms round my neck, enwrapping me in a scent I had never smelt before, then let herself slither into the boat:

beneath her groin, beneath her gluteal muscles, her body was that of a fish, covered in minute scales of blue and mother-of-pearl and ending in a forked tail which was slowly beating the bottom of the boat. She was a Siren.

And thereafter she

lay on her back with head resting on crossed hands, showing with serene immodesty a delicate down under her armpits, drawn-apart breasts, perfectly shaped loins; from her arose what I have wrongly called a scent but was more a magic smell of the sea, of youthful voluptuousness.

She spoke and after her smile and smell I was submerged by the third and greatest of charms, that of her voice. It was slightly guttural, veiled, reverberating with innumerable harmonies; behind the words could be sensed the lazy surf of summer seas, last spray rustling on the beach, winds passing on lunar waves...

Did anyone actually witness that wreckage of bones and flesh on Sirenum scopuli? Was it only gruesome destruction that took place on those shores? Might a siren's love simply be rough love? For while all sirens and mermaids embody the purest form of temptation—the unattainable woman in a myriad of ways: sex, sea, supernatural—it's not fair to assume that all are cruel. Perhaps they are just finicky in whom they choose to love, how they seduce, and whom they drive to merciless ruin.

As I see it, the siren—whether perched on a rocky Grecian cliff or folded into a plywood box for a music video—can sing the songs men most crave to hear, but I think she really sings for women, or at least would like to. I think the sirens were frustrated and angry because their melodies were intended for women's ears and because women were rarely found upon the high-rolling seas in the age of Homer. Perhaps they lashed out with their voices because of loneliness. They may have craved the sound of other high voices responding to theirs. Maybe they were furious that all these sailors left their wives behind, and thus they aimed to thwart their efforts to return. Perhaps they felt that Penelope, wife of the long-absent Odysseus, deserved better.

Whatever the sirens' intention, I suspect that a boat full of women could be ravished by the sound of the sirens and still pass by unharmed. No need to push wax into our ears and tie our arms and legs to the ship's mast. We wouldn't need to do anything so pompous and theatrical. Instead, we could all put on our swimsuits and join them in song. We would wave cheerfully as we sailed by, and the sirens would wave back. And with that idea in mind, I drove out to the beach on the first day I got my driver's license, *What if I'm a mermaid in these jeans...* playing on the tape deck and ocean fog still rolling in like slow-spilling milk. The hills as gold as ever, the foghorn still issuing its melancholy warning to boats no one could see.

3

You Might BE A SELKIE

...I took my stand before
A young seal lying on the shore;
And called on her to dance with me.
And it seemed hardly strange when she
Stood up before me suddenly,
And shed her black and sheeny skin;
And smiled, all eager to begin...
And I was dancing, heel and toe,
With a young maiden, white as snow,
Unto a crazy violin.

WILFRED WILSON GIBSON, "THE DANCING SEAL"

My mermaidenry was swimming along—always with an improving stroke and fueling an increasing desire for solitude and adventure. I found both in the city. I took the bus into San Francisco several afternoons a week. Crossing the Golden Gate Bridge, you had to decide between two dramatic views: to your right was the endless Pacific and steep headlands, to your left, the entirety of the postcard-perfect city skyline flanked by sailboats in the bay. Passengers on the bus always settled on one view. Nature lovers inevitably stared out to sea; everyone else eyed the skyscrapers. I watched both in equal measure, turning my head back and forth like a diligent watchguard. Both city and sea were oceans—just two different kinds.

Once in the city, I began spending a lot of my time at the San Francisco aquarium watching the dolphins. I wasn't a freak about it— I never wore sequined mermaid sweatshirts or pressed my face up to the glass—I simply liked being alone in this building, and the dim blue light of the aquarium brought me into a pleasant state of mind. For hours I could meander past fish tanks, admire seahorses, and pet velvety stingrays in the Touching Tidepool. The dolphins were always the highlight, though. Sitting on carpeted bleachers, listening to little kids ooh and aah as the dolphins cut through the turquoise water like slick torpedoes, feeling the levity in their stroke, seeing their round black eyes laugh at me laughing at them—nothing beat the dolphins. The blue of their painted tank seemed brighter to me than the rest.

Over time, I had developed an exclusive relationship with these dashing swimmers. They embodied the archetypal in-shape mermaid. I admired their muscle tone. I wanted to weigh however much they weighed. I thought about this as I drank hot tea and walked outdoors for some fresh air, towards the exhibits I rarely frequented: the otters, the seabirds, the seals.

Jasmine tea in my mouth, I tried to absorb how fat the seals were. It's all they were—long bundles of chub, shark treats, cute creatures surprisingly vulnerable in their heft. I was mesmerized by their bulk, and I couldn't help but notice how seal shoulders, when they shift beneath mounds of thick flesh, are things of incomparable beauty. Have you ever watched a seal climb out of the water onto a rock? Watched it lumber its body ashore? The two shelves of bone sway beneath the skin's surface like the hips of an extra slow belly dancer.

Dolphins suddenly seemed a little... hyper to me. I took another sip of tea, captivated by these giant seals lounging in front of me.

THE DARK GRAY of a seal's skin has undertones of rose and peachy-gold, and its form is undeniably womanly. Melancholy and matronly, the Atlantic gray seal especially is associated with the selkie, also called silkie, selchie, or roanne, a sister to the mermaid; both are women of the sea. Never a creature of fish-scaled extraction, the selkie swims as a seal in water and stands as a woman on land. Her mood and appearance are weightier than those of a mermaid; her deep-sea cadence rolls sober and slow. Grand dame of the high northern seas, the selkie exudes aquatic nobility and grace.

I have a good friend named Mitten who I think may be a selkie. I've always suspected this. The star of the high-school swim team, she smelled of chlorine, and her hair always hung in soaked strands down her back. She was compact and fit, her body wrapped in softness, with a generous rounding of the hips. Her limpid eyes were enormous and dark, eerily slow and always steady in their gaze, and her skin and hair always looked to be saturated with almond oil. Her eyelashes were very long; her hands and feet were small.

Envisioning her little hands as flipper tips was easy—they barely worked. She could hardly hold a pencil to write, and I always fought the urge to pull her fingers apart, separate their shovel-scoop tightness. She once told me that a piano teacher, employed by her father for a three-week stint when she was six years old, had felt the same way. She would rub emollient lotion all over my friend's little hands and rub them vigorously, cup them together, and blow into the hollow they made, trying to stoke warmth and dexterity. She massaged each knuckle and joint and gently tried to spread her fingers flat against the piano keys. They could not separate themselves and reach beyond a single ivory key, however, and, on her last day, the piano teacher sighed and said, "Octaves, my dear mitten-hands, are not for you." Hence the name Mitten.

To this day, Mitten's walk hints at a waddle. You can imagine her moving on a single powerful limb but not walking down a city street in pointy shoes and a skirt, balancing on two bone-pillared stilts.

Just as dolphins and seals surely play together in the sea, it figures that a seventeen-year-old mermaid would be drawn to a seventeen-year-old selkie—natural friends inexplicably drawn to each other. Mitten and I were inseparable.

The selkie as a woman is plain—lovely, though, as windswept prairie grass.

It was late afternoon, and we had spent the day together at Stinson Beach, a wide swath of sand and surf just off California's Highway 1 that is famous for its great white shark attacks. So popular with the whites, in fact, that girls who surfed weren't allowed in the water when they had their period. It was an unspoken rule, and it existed for two reasons. The first reason was the thinking of men: the blood brought sharks. But the second was a woman's understanding of the sea: blood calls to blood, and once the waves have yours, you belong to them.

I never viewed this as a bad thing.

The place was crowded with screeching seagulls hovering over the remnants of picnic lunches and brown bags. Lying on my side, I watched Mitten from the corner of my eye as she walked across the

dry sand to the wet, her black swimsuited body moving in a straight line towards the surf. Pelicans flew overhead, and I, as always, saluted them with mock formality.

She pushed through the salty water, parting the black-and-white webbed foam with her calves and kicking through ocean spray. I could see the water slapping and sloshing against her legs, and I could feel that frothy, whipped-egg-white texture of sea foam on my own skin as I imagined it on hers. Because it was late September, the ocean was spread beneath a metallic glaze, a sheet of silver flecked with rust and blue. Mitten's silhouette carved the smallest of triangles in the ocean, the farthest tip being her torso and the angular streams behind her garlands of broken water.

I watched as she began to swim against the strong, cold current, and it was not long before her head dipped beneath a little swell and she was gone. I lay on my back once more, closed my eyes, and felt the sun press its white warmth onto my slightly burnt cheeks. I must have dozed off, for when I looked out to the horizon again, the sun had knelt to water's edge and, steady and hot, prepared to extinguish itself in the Pacific. The light it yielded was plain and broad, casting thin shadows behind the sandy pampas grass, and the sea had emptied

◄ A selkie is a woman on land and a seal in the water, but never both at the same time.

itself of bathers and surfers. When the sun finally went under, it did so with a faint rattle, and the wind picked up noticeably.

I strained my eyes to find my friend. When I finally located her small dot of a head, there was not just one but now two. Weaving back and forth, in and out of breaking wavelets and still smaller swells, were two slick and glossy black balls, both catching and reflecting gold pools of moist light from their tops. These silhouetted heads spun around each other, drawing close and pulling back, plunging under the water's surface and suddenly reappearing; holding still in what seemed to be moments of mutual appreciation and tranquil courtship. This playful dance lasted for quite some time. Not until the hot peach light in the sky had vanished and twilight had descended, staining the sky and sea a deep lilac, did I lose sight of the two little heads.

I sat cross-legged on my beach towel, a blanket wrapped around my shoulders as the evening's chill came on, and waited for my friend's return. I had, of course, expected her to be in company. Surely she had just met some wet-suited swimmer guy? I assumed that once the watery couple had dried off and dressed, we three would retreat to the Sandcastle food kiosk just down the street. She would giggle and chirp in the embrace of this new fellow, and I would eat oysters, drink ginger ale, and listen to the details of their affair, which had clearly started off just swimmingly. But when she emerged from the ocean, she was alone.

She began to gather her things together in a nonchalant manner as I waited impatiently for her to speak.

"And who was that?" I finally burst out.

"Who was who?" Mitten replied in her mellow, singsong voice.

"The person you were with, the dancing head! You two were out there forever."

She paused, then answered slowly, "I wasn't with any person."

"Yes you were, yes you were—I couldn't even tell which one was you. All I could see were two black balls bouncing around on the water. Who was the guy? Why aren't you telling me?" Pause, "I totally saw you."

She pulled her dark, wavy hair back into a snug bun and gave me one of her long, soft stares. Her brown eyes suddenly seemed a little too brown, and they possessed, just then, a hitherto unseen quality: knowledge. She knew something I didn't. She wiggled into her jeans, buttoned the last button, slipped on her beaded flip-flops, and placed a dangling dentalium shell earring in each of her earlobes before turning back to me and saying, "Really, I wasn't with a person. I played with a seal for a little while is all, one who lives nearby, over in Agate Cove."

IF A SELKIE IS CAUGHT, she is said to make an excellent wife: handsome and dutiful, mindful of both children and husband. But to catch her is no easy thing. It involves either a certain heartlessness or blinded passion, for the man who commits the act will be exposed to unrestrained wailing, said to sear through both heart and night, a cry that wrings the gut because it is so human, so bitter, pitiful, and pained.

To capture her, then, requires immunity to tears and raw lament. But that kind of immunity is rewarded.

To possess a selkie is to lay claim to a woman with no interest in the human world beyond you and your offspring. According to most legends, once a selkie realizes that her chances of being returned to the sea are nil, she accepts both capture and captor, moving quickly into wifely action. A dress is put on, an apron too; dinner is prepared and children are born; boots are repaired and fires are stoked in the potbellied stove. She's not concerned with human parties or gossip, for her mind is occupied with the lost feeling of ocean currents pressing against her fur coat, flippers, and strong, rounded breast. Her mind is empty of human thoughts, filled with the sound of the sea. On dry land she becomes an attentive wife, though one bereft of zestful spirit and soul.

Many children have been born with seal blood in their veins.

Other women don't understand her, dislike her, and complain to their husbands about the aloof and unfriendly "looker" who always stares out to sea. After nodding their heads obligingly in response to their wives' grumbling, the husbands leave the house and walk out in unspoken search of the gray-eyed, dark-haired seal-woman. Congregated en masse in the town pub, these men look up from pints of brown ale and watch her walk by the steamy glass window. Conversation wanes and all eyes fix on the shapely figure of the mysterious newcomer shrouded in a blue wool dress with a grocery bag carried on the hip.

The selkie as a woman is plain—lovely, though, as windswept prairie grass and clear glass Christmas ornaments sitting in a wood bowl. She is without freckles or blushed complexion; her face is uniformly pale and highlighted along the cheekbones by smudges of unpolished silver—skin shined up by the salty sea. Her jaw is square, but her cheeks are round, her eyebrows are dark and distinctive, arching in two thick, angular crescents. Above her pale lips, soft down resides; her nose is aquiline. Her breasts swell in a firm mound, neither yielding nor doughy, but shapely from a life spent pushing through the sea—a chest sculpted like the hull of a sailboat.

Beneath her stout waist, wide hips curve, and her near-black hair falls in heavy waves past her tailbone. Unlike the other women in town, she does not pull her hair back and wrap it in bands and braids; she lets it hang loose, tamed only by a single ivory clip above her left ear. Those more critical of the seal-woman suspect her of being dumb, for most of the time she doesn't respond to questions asked of her and she is uninterested in all things social. Those more intrigued, however, find in her a creature loftier than the hennish women about town; they sense within her silence a power and otherworldy mystique that they themselves cannot relate to but admire.

But how does one catch a selkie? And how does one keep such a strange creature in a dry, blandly human environment?

An act of theft is required: her skin must be stolen and hidden where she will never find it. Scandinavian legend holds that each year on Twelfth Night (the evening of January 6, the feast of the Epiphany, which is the concluding day of medieval Christmas), the selkies disrobe. Like seals that sunbathe on ocean rocks and hidden beaches, selkies too crave the feel of earth underfoot: cool stone, dirt beneath bare-skinned feet, and the earthy sound of drums. The selkies swim into rocky caves and upon beachfronts to shed their hides and dance naked till dawn, beneath the light of the moon.

Rumor of such events gets round, and many young men have lurked behind boulders and sand dunes with the goal of snagging a skin and, in turn, a woman more mysterious and lovely than any town girl could wish to be. One of the boys who succeeded in such coat theft is remembered in Scottish legend. After the sun went down, the young man went to the sea and crouched between some tight rocks, waiting for the seals to come. They soon did, in great number, and he beheld the most beautiful woman he had ever laid eyes upon stepping out of her skin. Though she was somewhat plain in appearance, her black eyes and naked limbs bathed in moonlight stole his breath away. Once she was consumed by the pleasure of dancing, he crept up to the fur, took it, and returned to his hiding place.

Morning light rose, and the seals returned to their skins. The black-eyed woman, however, could not find hers. She looked frantically for it, wringing her hands in fear of the sun's first rays, until suddenly she caught her skin's scent in the arms of the boy. She ran to him and pleaded with him to return the fur to her. She wept. He remained stoic and, turning his back to her, walked away.

She had no choice but to follow, and thus she became his wife. His affection for her was politely returned, and though they got along well enough and had several children, she never overcame her desire to return to the sea. It is said that she would often steal away to the nearby sandbar, and a large seal would make his appearance. The two would speak anxiously in a language no one understood. Craving her first husband, the seal-man she was forced to leave behind, she asked how the children were, wondered if a spare sealskin had ever been found, implored him never to stop his visits to her.

Years passed and nothing changed, until one day her son happened upon the sealskin beneath a stack of hay—or corn, or in some versions locked up in a great wooden chest—and proudly brought the skin to his mother to show it off. Her eyes glistened with rapture, and in a burst of frenzied joy she grabbed the skin from her young son's hands and made ready to dash to the waves. Her pace was slowed for a brief moment, however, when she stared upon her children, whom she was about to abandon. She paused and hastily hugged each, kissing their heads in turn; she then said goodbye and wasted no time in flying out the door.

The selkie's seal husband congratulated her on her quick escape, and the two dove deep and swam away. She was a seal once more and at home in the sea.

Motherless children, desolate husbands, cold kitchens—many stories of the selkie paint her as one who heartlessly leaves all this behind. But not all of them do. Many selkies have been pained when severing their connection to dry life. An Icelandic selkie, upon recovering her lost skin, once said, "This I want, and yet I want it not, seven children have I at the bottom of the sea, seven children have I as well here above."

She chose to leave her seven dry, but from that day on, whenever her landbound husband went out to fish, she swam around his boat and tears ran from her eyes. She blessed him in ways she could. He began to catch many fish; his rope nets became heavier than they ever had been before as she swam under the little boat, catching fish in her claws and placing each one in his net. And when his children walked along the beach by their house, a seal swam beside them, throwing colorful fish and pretty shells at their bare feet.

SELKIE SIGHTINGS have occurred for a long time. As David Thomson, author of the wonderful little book *The People of the Sea*, explains, legends of the selkie and her closeness to humans were once common knowledge and the subject of nightly storytelling in coastal villages. But recently, elders have become self-conscious about their old legends, humbled by the younger generation's scorn, and their eagerness to share them has faded. "The link with their forefathers," writes Thomson, "the passing on of history, genealogy, legend and belief by word of mouth was beginning to weaken even then [late

› *Mermaidenly women are linked by the sisterhood of the sea.*

1940s], as skills such as rope-making and thatching are weakening now." Belief in the seal-folk, once as tight as handmade rope and brought to use every day, has loosened and come undone.

Cynicism has replaced open-mindedness, and with the passing of each elder, something of the selkie is lost. Yet there was a time when trust in the seal-woman was intrinsic to one's view of the world, when mysterious women were assumed to have aquatic origins and no one batted an eye or said a harsh word about them.

Embraced as family, selkies cooked and ate meals in the kitchen and played with the children—or rather, the children played with them. Sneaking up behind them, the kids would flatten their hands and, with a pointed thrust, hit the backs of women's knees to find out whether they had two normal legs or whether their lower halves fell into a seal's thick flank and flipper. These selkies in the kitchen were always a mystery to their families, but they were regarded as kin nevertheless.

With so many men stealing sealskins and marrying selkies in Ireland, Scotland, and shores beyond, many children have been born with seal blood in their veins. There are families in these countries today that trace matrilineal ancestry to the seal-women and, as a result, are believed to be safe from drowning and blessed with good fishing luck. No storm will turn their boat; no wave will push them under tempestuous, white-capped seas. Their nets will always be heaped high with silver, flapping fish. When seals are considered to be not simply animals but *family*, hunting them is judged a very grave crime. No one with a selkie in his or her ancestral tree would ever lay harm to a seal as it sunbathed on the shore or swam through the sea—just as one would never drive a harpoon shaft or bullet through the bosomy chest of one's beloved great aunt while she strolled through her flower garden or drank tea by the fire.

And not to be overlooked: there are male selkies in the sea as well, famous for their infatuation with human women. Many a child has been sired by a tremendous gray seal-man.

The famous ballad "The Great Selkie o' Suleskerry" tells of the tragic consequences that sometimes arise from the union of a sea-bound selkie and a land-living woman.

I heard a mother lull her bairn,
and aye she rocked, and aye she sang.
She took so hard upon the verse
that the heart within her body rang.

"O, cradle row, and cradle go,
and aye sleep well, my bairn within;
I ken not who thy father is,
nor yet the land that he dwells in."

And up then spake a grey selchie
as aye he woke her from her sleep,
"I'll tell where thy bairn's father is:
he's sittin' close by thy bed feet.

"I am a man upon the land;
I am a selchie on the sea,
and when I'm far frae ev'ry strand,
my dwelling is in Sule Skerry.

"And foster well my wee young son,
aye for a twal'month and a day,
and when that twal'month's fairly done,
I'll come and pay the nourice fee."

And when that weary twal'month gaed,
he's come tae pay the nourice fee;

he had ae coffer fu' o' gowd,

and anither fu' o' the white money.

"Upon the skerry is thy son;

upon the skerry lieth he.

Sin thou would see thine ain young son,

now is the time tae speak wi' he."

"But how shall I my young son know

when thou ha' ta'en him far frae me?"

"The one who wears the chain o' gowd,

'mang a' the selchies shall be he.

"And thou will get a hunter good,

and a richt fine hunter I'm sure he'll be;

and the first ae shot that e'er he shoots

will kill baith my young son and me."

Joan Baez did a cover of this old ballad, and though the sadness of it was clear, a bone-soaking sorrow that filled my bedroom, it was long before I really understood it. The confusion came, in part, because not all versions of the song include the final verse. When the woman's new husband, the hunter, comes home with his day's hunting bounty, and she reaches for the two dead seals to begin their skinning, she discovers the gold chain around the neck of the small one. As she realizes that the seal pup is her very son, the ancient melody concludes:

"Alas, alas this woeful fate

This weary fate that's been laid for me.

And once or twice she sobbed and sighed,

An' her tender heart did brak' in three."

Like the brooding gray coast itself—haunting home of the selkies—many of the tales surrounding them are of a wistful sort. Their stories begin in lament, in tears shed for a lost sealskin and all that goes with it. Yet, more often than not, the stories end with a reversal of loss: the man who captured the selkie to keep as his own grieves when she leaves. But there are exceptions.

From the island of Sanday, one of the northern Orkney Islands, comes the story "One Spared to the Sea." In it a man named Willie Westness from Over-the-Watter was digging for bait in a sandy bay. His pail filled quickly, and as he still had time before the tide came in, he decided to look for driftwood up the shore. It was then that he heard "the cry from the rocks—a moan like that of a woman in pain swelling into a loud, strange sound and dying into a sort of sob."

Following the distressed sound, Westness stealthily crawled towards a pile of rocks and looked down. Beneath him lay a big mother seal and her newborn pup. As she caught sight of the tall, gaunt man with the tarnished pail at his side, she heaved her great bulk into the water. Her pup, however, lay helpless at the man's feet. Westness picked it up, allowing it to nuzzle his hand, and thought to himself of how he would keep it.

The mother seal quickly realized his intention and began to "clumsily back out of the water to lie moaning at the edge, her round eyes full of tears." With this the pup took cue and gazed at the man's face with "soft blurred brown eyes," and as Westness noticed how its little round head was just "like a child's," he placed the pup at the sea's edge, whispering, "Ach, selkie, take thee bairn and be gone wi' ye!"

Nine years later Westness had his own family of four. The three youngest had chosen a sunny day to gather cockles. They ventured to a place that their father had warned them against because of the deep, strong high tide that swept in (though in the same breath he made the mistake of praising the very fine quality of the cockles located there). Promising themselves that they would be speedy in their collecting, the children crossed over and began to gather. Yet when their pails were full and they turned to go, the tide began flowing in fast.

In no time at all, the cold water was to their knees and rising steadily. They pressed themselves against the rocks and began to cry and scream, when suddenly they heard soft singing beside them. Two women in gray cloaks had come up behind them. "Come away bairns, come away. It will soon be too late," said the elder of the two. She took their hands, while the second woman took their buckets, and they walked straight into the water. By the time they neared the other side, the tide was swirling around their necks and, had it not been for the warm hands holding theirs, the children surely would have drowned.

"All's well," said the woman, and her plump face smiled down at them in a kindly fashion. "Now take thee father a word from me. Remember now, say to thee father, Willie Westness, to mind a day when he digged for lugworm at the geo, nine summers gone. And say to him that one spared to the sea is three spared to the land."

Their stories begin

They turned and ran home, repeating the whole way "one spared to the sea is three spared to the land." Once they had reached the top of the cliff, they turned to look back.

in lament, in tears shed

for a lost sealskin.

The tide was high over the rocks, and the currents battled in a frothed fury, swells slapping and sloshing against each other. The gray-cloaked women, however, were nowhere to be seen. Only a pair of swimming seals moved along the water's surface: two sleek blades cutting through the afternoon surf.

WOMEN ON LAND, seals in the water: selkies are not so much seen as suspected. Unlike the mermaid whose fish-tailed appearance leaves no doubt in the eyes of the observer, the selkie is more subtle in her transformations. Never a being of halves—part human, part animal—selkies are one or the other.

Whereas the mermaid has been labeled by some as an example of zoological error, wishful thinking blended with misidentification, or scientific observation gone awry, the selkie has never been explained away as anything other than herself. She is a woman who has never been called sea cow, dugong, or manatee, all creatures that some people consider the "origins" of the mermaid myth. She is just a seal in the sea and a woman on the land, pure and simple.

I'VE WONDERED if husbands don't feel a bit frustrated not knowing their selkie wives very well. Receiving little affection and suspecting that their wives have not only second husbands in watery realms but children too, what does the selkie offer them that is so satisfying, that eclipses any need for genuine human intimacy? Is the selkie's silence valued and appreciated? Perhaps it is her low-maintenance domesticity? Having snared the seal-woman as a hunter catches a spotted deer, does the husband relish his prize and mastery over another living thing? Is that what fuels the interest?

When one dives into the powers of symbolism and allegory, control emerges as a central issue in the selkie legend. Once the man picks up the shed sealskin, the selkie is powerless. The skin stolen from her represents freedom and autonomy; the open sea is symbolic of her world of opportunity, frivolous play, and boundless possibility.

Selkie tales often illuminate women's view of marriage. In the days of popular selkie lore, marriage was normally imposed on a young girl (certainly the case when the match was arranged); it was a state of affairs beyond her control, and she was expected simply to resign herself to it, to make the best of it. A woman can be a "good" wife without, as the selkie shows, being an affectionate one, and thus she may stare out at the open sea and lust for her former life without upsetting the (probably now "old-fashioned") duties and expectations of wedlock.

The "lock" in wedlock is quite precise in this case. It is the selkie's husband who holds and hides her fate. The key to her freedom—her sealskin—dangles from his belt or lies buried in a place of his choosing. Selkie tales define matrimony as institutionalized capture, as a woman's indentured servitude to a man.

Perhaps this definition no longer applies. To move forward in time for a moment, this past summer was filled with profound festivities: engagement parties, weddings, and baby showers, accompanied by glasses of chardonnay, small sandwiches, girlish conversation, and frocks. Meaty topics, however, were discussed, especially why we friends were getting married. Marriage is no longer the skeleton key to sex, financial security, and family; all those things may easily be had without vows, legal sanction, and expensive receptions replete with champagne and black-and-white photographs. So what was it about the act that still warmed us?

We were all eager to "shed our sealskins" for the simple reason that, aside from love and all that, we no longer had to. No skin was stolen—we stepped out of it of our own accord. Society's expectations of marriage have largely changed, nuptials being optional rather than mandatory, and we felt empowered, not weakened, by our decisions to wed. It was about going public, so to speak. Marriage today is, in theory, not about feeling that one's life has been locked irrevocably into place but rather, as one friend said, it is a thing that "should give

you bigger wings to fly with." We choose to marry, and we keep our sealskins folded neatly in our own underwear drawers.

Or do we?

It was a little past midnight when a friend of mine phoned. She had given birth to her first child, a baby girl, a few weeks before. Her husband was away on business; her two dogs had been barking all day, envious of the baby, who received so much of her attention; the whole day had consisted of general chaos, overwhelming and exhausting. Totally unlike the glamorous life of art galleries and dinner parties she had enjoyed a year ago.

"If someone handed me a plane ticket to Paris, and I could just walk away from all of this, right now, I'd be pretty hard-pressed to decide not to go," she said in a dry voice, and added, "I know it's just a bad moment."

Even if the sealskin is within reach, it doesn't always fit the way it used to. But it's still there—the skin, the option to run, to explore other things. Like having the ocean in your backyard and choosing to visit only the water's edge, just allowing your toes to dip into a life you left.

‹ *Mermaids have, on occasion, been caught*
in the embrace of an unwanted lover.

I REMAINED THOROUGHLY mystified by Mitten's selkie ways. We went to the beach many more times together that summer, nearly every weekend, and sometimes, when she didn't have to work at the coffee shop, we drove out on weekday evenings too. We'd hop into her old yellow Volvo and listen to Joni Mitchell. Windows down and warm wind blowing through them, making our hair crazy; the stack of silver bracelets on her wrists jangled with every Highway 1 snake-curve bend, and sometimes, around dusk, a herd of white deer sprinkled themselves in the open meadows. Catching sight of these animals of soft fur and brown eye was about as fantastic as finding unicorns among the redwoods. We'd slow the car down, pull over in one of the gravel turnouts, and watch the ethereal creatures munch grass.

When the crescent moon was out, tipped low in the blue-dust sky drizzled with diamond-fleck stars, my heart slipped along the contours of absolute enchantment. It was like a scene from the *Nutcracker*, set upon a stage that swept out as far as the eye could see and was enhanced by the feeling of "real life," of knowing that life was actually this good; no costumes or makeup would be removed at the end of the show. You could just sit in the car and smell summer grass and watch white deer nibble their floral dinner while Joni Mitchell sang "Carey" to you. *Come on down to the Mermaid Café and I will buy you a bottle of wine/And we'll laugh and toast to nothing and smash our empty glasses down . . .*

Once on the beach, I would set up camp: beach blanket spread, blue jeans off and neatly folded, thermos pitched in the sand, picnic basket placed just so, flip-flops into my canvas bag. Before I had even unfurled my towel, Mitten was walking towards the surf. By the time my toes were wiggling and burrowing in the sand, she was swimming.

It was rare that she swam by herself. Often she was accompanied by that second black ball in the water, sometimes more. One afternoon there looked to be a good dozen or so of the little heads out there. They surrounded my friend (at least I think they did; it was always tough to discern her head among theirs) and circled her like dancers around a maypole. When the seagulls and pelicans plunged from the sky in a throng of winged chaos, the little heads joined them in what must have been a feeding frenzy, a swarm of unfortunate herring being chowed.

When she returned to the dry sand, sometimes an hour after she had left, she offered no details of her long swim. How could she endure the freezing water for so long? The temperatures dipped below 50 degrees, and everyone knew hypothermia set in fast along this cold piece of coast. She didn't wear a wetsuit, didn't rub down her body with grease. How could she stand it? She was a little plump, but surely not plump enough to withstand the iced currents and frigid upwelling of the northern Pacific Ocean without insulating protection.

I pulled a bottle of cabernet sauvignon, sneaked out of the parents' liquor cabinet, and two plastic cups from the picnic basket.

"Are you going to be a seal again for Halloween this year?" I asked.

"Probably," she replied, reaching for her cup.

The cork popped with a dull *pumph,* and I poured some wine into each cup, a tad more than halfway. Her seal costume won every contest, in every club, every year. It consisted of a shiny, steel-colored unitard with a zipper up the back and a high neck as well as a pair of diving flippers she had painted with gray acrylic paint and silver glitter. Around her neck she wore a string of black pearls that her father had given her on her sixteenth birthday, and she put loads of styling gel into her hair, making it look glossy, wet, and slick. She made an excellent seal.

Selkies are not so much seen as suspected.

I fiddled with a strand of my hair and picked some opalescent polish off my toenail before finally, after months of inching towards the inquiry, finding the nerve to ask, "Are you a selkie?"

Asking point blank granted me an immediate surge of relief. I felt as though an overblown balloon was allowing itself to deflate. I, of course, expected her to say, "Well, yep, Mandy, I am."

"What's a selkie?"

I was thunderstruck. Could she really not know? After all this? After I had felt so sure that this mermaid had met her match?

"You *don't* know what a selkie is?"

She shook her head no and swallowed a mouthful more of wine.

I lay down on my stomach and kicked the blanket over my calves. "They are the seal-women," I said, "seals in water and women on land. They come up sometimes, on the rocks to dance, and when they do, they take off their sealskin coats. Men will steal their skins and make the selkies their wives. Without their skins, they can't return home, so they make a new one, one above the sea."

Mitten was paying attention.

I finished my wine. "Yeah, they belong to two worlds, but they're happiest in the water. They have human kids, though, and those children have seal blood. Even if they're not all selkie, I suppose they're part. They must be part. Hey, you should ask your dad more about your mom, Mitts."

Mitten shifted her gaze from my mouth to the sea. She was moving very slowly, and her breathing was deep and low, almost labored. She had never met her mother, this I knew. Apparently her father, when he was a young man, had vacationed at Brighton Beach along the southeastern shore of England and had met a ravishingly beautiful woman named Morgen. The two fell madly in love, as he tells it, and spent an unforgettable summer by the beach, drinking and dancing and making love at all hours. By the end of July, Mitten's mother was pregnant, and her parents, both very poor at the time, rented a one-bedroom flat and lived frugally, saving all their money for diapers and blankets and stuffed-bear toys. Mitten's mother worked part-time as a lifeguard, and her father was a bartender in the corner pub.

After the baby was born, a brawny spring storm pounded the small city, and the tide swooped in very high. Mitten's father relished this part of the tale and always told it with shameless drama. He puffed his cigar and made smooth currents in the air with the fragrant blue smoke.

"The tide came in like a brand-new lake," he said. "It just covered the town and sat stagnant for days on end. There was seaweed rotting on the water and dead fish belly-up, floating like those buoys with the white tops. Yes, girly girls, it was a real mess."

The high tide smothered the beach and boardwalk shops and did not roll back again until the day Mitten's mother vanished. Woman and tide left together.

When he came home, the baby girl was alone in her crib, and lined up in the refrigerator were giant glass jugs filled with rich milk, enough to feed the child for several weeks. Her father said that the milk was so thick and fatty he had to water it down before giving the baby a bottle. "It poured out like oily yogurt," he told us.

"Do you know what your mom looked like?" I asked.

"A little. My dad showed me the only picture he has of her, only. . . " she started to laugh sheepishly, "he waited to show me the picture till I was older 'cause it's a bit x-rated."

For the life of me I could not envision Mitten's tweed-wearing father engaged in any risqué activities.

"Like sex pictures?" I asked, a little stunned.

"No! Not at all!" She filled her cup to the brim with wine and took a deep quaff. Color came to her cheeks and her eyes turned glassy; her breathing evened out. "Not at all. Dad used to be into photography; that's why he was spending his summer on the coast. He liked to take pictures of horizons. He was doing this whole project about horizon lines: flatlands, ocean lines, skylines. Anyway, one day he was walking along the beach by the rocks and the tidepools, and he sees this beautiful lady sitting naked on, like, a boulder or something. She was crying and really upset." More wine; Mitten lay down beside me and propped herself up on both elbows.

"He asked her what was wrong, and she told him that someone had stolen her clothes and she couldn't go back home without them." She giggled, "Dad still says, 'Meeting your mother, honey, was like bumping into a washed-up angel.' He asked if he could take her photo, and she said yes. That's how they met, the first words they spoke. But she covered herself in the photo. I mean, it's not *really* x-rated. She's kind of balled up and shy looking. Anyway, Dad took her home. He loved her so much till she left. Even after that too."

Evidently, Mitten's mother had finally found her clothes.

Yemaya
ON THE BEACH

...Do I dare to eat a peach?
I shall wear white flannel trousers, and walk upon the beach.
I have heard the mermaids singing, each to each.

I do not think they will sing to me.

I have seen them riding seaward on the waves
Combing the white hair of the waves blown back
When the wind blows the water white and black.

T.S. ELIOT, "THE LOVE SONG OF J. ALFRED PRUFROCK"

$\mathcal{M}$ost people have a turning point when they feel they can and want to take care of something beyond themselves. For me it began with tomatoes. It took me a while to get there, however, and if it hadn't been for my introduction to the motherly attributes of the great Yemaya, it might never have happened.

As our teenage years drew to a close and our bright twenties loomed on the horizon, Mitten remained as much of a selkie as ever. The day after graduation she turned down a swim-team scholarship at the local state university to travel around England and visit some unknown cousins. Her relatives had been sending enthusiastic postcards all year, each one portraying a rugged seascape and stone wall with only a few words written on the back. Usually no more than *Sweetheart: you will just know you're home.*

When I dropped Mitten off at the airport, she was wearing a charcoal-gray raincoat, her black pearl necklace, and a knitted blue dress. A red cap on her head and thick mascara on her lashes—she looked incredible, sultry and all vavoom. I didn't expect to see her again for a long time; surely a girl as gorgeous as she would have too much fun in London to merit any quick return home. She might even have too much fun on the plane, if the admiring looks of the entire Cornwall wall soccer team lined up at the ticket counter were any indication.

I too remained ensconced in my mermaid ways. A newly minted eighteen-year-old, I felt the whole world was my oyster, and I was coming into my mermaid own. Dragonfly-blue skirts, clingy silk tank tops that hung off the shoulder, dangling pearl earrings, beaded vintage sweaters, green eye shadow, sequined sandals, glossy lip balm, jeans tight as a tail—I was completely outfitted in "merm." I decorated my hair with abalone barrettes and a single cobalt hair extension that fell from scalp past cheek to breastbone.

I was having dinner with a woman from my painting class when, over a plate of king crab legs and papaya salad, we landed on the topic of mermaids. The woman, named Miranda, smelled strongly of gardenias. The scent of her caught in my throat, so much so that I instinctively washed it down with gulps of icy virgin margarita every few minutes. You could taste the flowers.

"Mermaids." Miranda's eyes became big and wide. She folded her arms on the rickety table and leaned towards me, ample bosom pouring over her forearms. Her ash-colored hair was streaked with white and piled up in a casual chignon, fastened with a chopstick. She wore a bright floral caftan, all blues and greens with blotches of yellow, stamens of magenta, and a pair of beaded earrings she had made herself. Miranda was a jewelry maker and self-proclaimed dharma bum. She sold trinkets out of her cream-colored 1966 Jaguar convertible, which had a vanity plate that read GODSS 1. Her eyes were rimmed in lilac, and her lipstick was a definite shade of brown, dull as weathered farm equipment.

"Oh honey, as soon as I got these," she said as she pushed her hands into her pillowy breasts and ran a finger beneath a turquoise bra strap, "I was just crawling for mermaids. It was a puberty thing. . . having to live with my dad, I needed that sleek little mermaid to be some kind of mom, a kinda role model, you see."

"A mom?" This was one version of mermaid love I wasn't acquainted with.

"You bet. Here I was. . ."—she stretched her arms overhead and shook out her heavy hair—"this little thing turning into a mother goddess made of all sexy curves. My pa just kept giving me basketballs and hockey jerseys for Christmas. They didn't even fit! You should've seen how those numbers spread across my chest!" She practically moaned with laughter. "He just sat there watching the television, drinking his can of beer. . . no idea his baby girl was becoming a sexy, sexy lady. Of course, I needed the mermaid." She winked at me and bit into a crab leg.

I took a sip of my margarita and thought about tequila.

"So the mermaid became like. . . a mom?" I asked incredulously. This defied everything sexy about the mermaid. I began seeing all my friends' mothers as mermaids, and this was not what I wanted.

"I don't mean some 'don't let that boy put his hand in your sweater' kind of mom. All disciplinary. I mean it in the larger sense, Candy-Mandy, I mean it as in she became a woman of inspiration and divine lesson."

These last words were spoken as gospel.

"Ah," I smiled, and nodded knowingly. "Gospel." I had no idea what she was talking about. Miranda threw a seed-pearl grin back at me (her teeth were tiny) and raised her salt-rimmed glass. We clinked—*to the mermaid!*—and ordered key lime pie for dessert.

"You know," Miranda leaned over and said in a husky whisper, "a mermaid can have any man."

Maybe not Fig, I thought to myself—we mermaids didn't swim deep enough. But when our waiter with the anchor tattoo on his wrist took our order and walked away, Miranda made that little mermaid sound in approval, that dolphin squeal of delight I knew all too well. And the waiter actually did look back.

"DIVINE LESSON": was it an overstatement? Of course mermaids *look* divine, but aside from the mer-god Oannes, I never quite thought of them as teachers per se. Mermaids are the lyrical reflections of human desire, powerful deities and symbols of womanly liberation; but mothers too? My personal mermaid love had always been rooted, more or less, in physical fascination. The extraordinary tail, the secret scales, the underwater skills: these were the comforts of my mermaidenry. Even when pondering her deeper shades of meaning—her feminist worth—I nevertheless fell back on the splashy drama of turning tail, on the mermaid's offer of escape, the enchantment of leaving humanity and legs behind.

But perhaps I was missing the ocean for the branches of coral. Was it possible that I hadn't tuned into the mermaid's full message? Could it be that I was missing some element belonging to the more mature mermaid? How and why did she resonate with other women? For instance, did the redhead standing at the bar in her Japanese tidal wave, woodcut-print pants, clamshell belt buckle, and shimmery halter top know that she was appealingly "merm"? Was she trying, or was she oblivious to her effect?

My gut instinct was to field the Mermaid as All Mother viewpoint with some suspicion. It was too fuzzy, too convenient, too grounded in contemporary New Age thinking to apply to mermaids of the past. More to the point, it was too monolithic an interpretation: as if all the mermaids of the world could be gathered and netted within one form of understanding. Perhaps I had read too many essays on how the mermaid and her watery realms were symbolic of amniotic fluid, birth, feminine darkness, castration anxiety, and impenetrable mystery, how the ocean is really just symbolic sex soup and the great mother presides. This view never did much for me, and it certainly never jibed with my interest in the mermaid.

Yet, listening to Miranda, it occurred to me that I might have been too hasty in my judgements, perhaps too young. The mermaid may never have felt like a mother to me, but she was a solid mentor. Who was I to draw the line between the two? Had I not had a mother of my own, perhaps I too would have crawled into the embrace of some matronly mermaid, would have excavated my secrets and sense of direction from her generous presence and nuanced myth. Mentor and mother: are they really so different?

It was a couple of years after my lunch with Miranda, when I was living in Seattle, that I came to better appreciate the mermaid's maternal qualities. I was sitting on a beach that looked out towards the snow-capped mountains of the Olympic Peninsula, on a calm, clear winter morning. Feet dry in the sand, empty of any irresistible siren's song, I watched a woman to my left.

She was a round woman dressed in crisp, bleached white from crocheted turban to Ked-covered toe. Her skin was the color of dark polished wood, carved curvy and full. Her arms were lifted up to the sky, and she was holding a bunch of grapes in each hand. With slow, deliberate moves, she drew the grapes down towards her face and—after kissing a mouthful, first right, then left— brought the grapes to her neck and dragged

First-time mothers-to-be

seek out Yemaya

when they are pregnant.

them slowly along her shoulders, allowing the waxy branches to pull through her hair. Combining the two bunches into one, she used both hands to carry the fruit down and back up each leg. Circling them around her thighs up to her belly and then kissing them once again, she set the grapes upon the small, lapping waves. At her feet a burning candle melted slowly—tiny flame flickering inside a clear glass column—and the grapes, lit white by the sun, began to roll on the water.

She proceeded to do the same with a coconut, a lime, a mango, some bananas, three or four lemons, and an apple. Each item was presented to the sea, grazing past her bare feet, with decorum. The

fruit began up high, illuminated by pale December light, and made its way down, in the cups of her brown palms, to the water, by a series of wide and generous spirals around her body.

I sat beside the remnants of a bonfire, driftwood still smoldering at noon, and watched this woman's prayers. Her white shawl fluttered in the chill breeze, and her ivory skirts whipped around her thick ankles like sails on the mast. She had a gold-plated tooth that caught the sun in a miniature blast of bright, and all in all, she resembled a blissful pirate-turned-angel grounded in oystershell sand. A woman in sharp contrast to the other beachgoers, dressed in dark coats, jeans, and ratted scarves slogging through wet sand while cutting a wide swath around "the woman doing the ritual."

The fruit bobbed near the woman's feet in a semicircle, like a group of excited children around a toy-giver. Silhouetted by mountains, a medley of fruit, and silvery water, the woman evoked impressions of fertility and ancient rites: a West Coast Venus clad in cotton. The solitary mango slowly drifted my way and came to a drunken halt before me, underscoring a feeling of connection to the woman and her worship. We were, it seemed, communing wordlessly by way of a cheerful line of floating fruit that paid attention to us both.

Her last round of invocations consisted not of fruit but of sand. She grabbed two fistfuls and followed that path around her neck and calves before throwing her final offering into the sea. After some

‹ *Women have long seen elements of their innermost selves in the mermaid.*

moments bent in thought, folded into a white ball upon the shore, the woman stood and returned to her canvas bag and her towel laid out by a driftwood log.

I waited until the feeling of sanctified space dissolved a little before taking my question to her. It was when a dog ran over and threw its sandy wet paws on her pristine skirts and when she laughed and sort of blessed the dog's head with pats and smiles and some vigorous scratching behind its ears that I walked over to her and sat down.

"Miss?"

"Yes, child?"

"*What was that?*" My question came out like a voice cast in a spell.

"I was worshipping my guardian spirit, Yemaya, spirit of the sea. We are given our own guardians." She untied the white scarf on her head. "You know the Santeria religion?"

I shook my head no.

She began wrapping aluminum foil around leftover apples. "It came over on the Middle Passage, came on the slave boats from the west coast of Africa. You see, it lived on rich and warm in the people's hearts even when they were dying terrible. When it's good out like this, I bring fruit to my guardian spirit, my *orisha*; she likes fruit. And I ask her things."

"Is she, is your guardian spirit . . . a mermaid?" I could nearly hear thunder in my ears, and my heart was racing.

"Yes. Well, yes, it is one of her manifestations. Yes, sometimes Yemaya is made manifest as a mermaid. Sometimes she wears seven skirts on land. She is the great nurturer of women and children, the almighty mother, and she has a blue-and-white fish tail." The woman gave me an open stare and smiled with a gentle lifting of her head. "Nothing is more beautiful than the great mother, Yemaya," said she, and I nodded in response.

Later that night at the University of Washington library, I learned that the exalted Yemaya is indeed viewed as a mother goddess of all oceans, the protector of women and children up and down the eastern coasts of the Americas and outlying islands. Celebrated and revered not only in the Pacific Northwest but also in Cuba, Puerto Rico, Trinidad, and other Caribbean islands as well as in Brazil. She is known in African-Caribbean traditions as Yemaya, Yemaja, Jemanja, Iemanja, and Ymoja; in Haiti she is called Agwe; and in New Orleans, La Balianne.

First-time mothers-to-be seek out Yemaya when they are pregnant. They write her letters asking for blessing and good luck in childbirth and toss them to the sea. Other followers celebrate their mermaid several times a year—in late December, in early February, and on the eve of the summer solstice. In Brazil, on December 31, little boats filled with flowers and perfume are set out on the sea as gifts. People toss bottles of champagne, flowers, crystals, soap, and the mermaid's favorite scents—sandalwood, tea rose, frangipani—into the sea as offerings. When melons are in season, they throw those in too, as Yemaya is rumored to have a sweet tooth. If the offerings are taken out with the tide, the mermaid has bestowed her blessing; if they are pushed back to the sand, she is dissatisfied and the hopes of her followers are dashed.

The colors of her tail, blue and white, inspire the dress of her adoring fans. Men and women in white skirts and slacks and blue belts, shirts, bandanas, and hats pay homage to their mermaid, at least annually, in various festivals. Doused with cologne, they drink sparkling wine under midnight skies and dance in celebration of their mermaid mother till morning, renewing their appreciation of oceanic faith. And like Sedna of the high North, Yemaya is viewed not only as powerful, but also as quite real and omnipresent in the modern day.

The summer passed with the sound of small waves lapping on the shores.

Mother of the Ocean and Mother of All Waters are two of Yemaya's signifiers. The latter name conjures up the episode wherein Yemaya gave birth to the world's waters. With each step and each turn in her sleep, springs and rivers broke through the earth's surface until the ground was moist and the plants began to grow. In other versions of the story, it is said that after being raped by her own son, Yemaya chose to die high on a mountaintop. And in her death, it was the bursting of her womb that brought floods and then oceans to the world. This story makes any cleansing dip in the sea a touch more visceral in its mermaid immediacy: the ocean's womblike quality becomes more than just metaphoric.

With cowrie shells strung around their necks and wrists—shells symbolic of Yemaya—women turn to the great mermaid not only when they are pregnant but also when they need help with infertility. Speaking to the waves, they tell of their own dreams of motherhood.

Many mermaids are mothers. But for Melusina, for example, motherhood was an afterthought, a side story to the tail. She continued to nurse her children, though, by moonlight and in spite of her cursed exile. Selkies are distant mothers—a little preoccupied, but nonetheless efficient. Yet Yemaya stands alone as the ultimate mermother. Not every mermaid has the maternal instinct, and many are mischievous, dangerous, and ferociously solo. But Yemaya offers that warmth, that soft and comforting tail to bury your head and sorrows in, your wishes and fears. She is revered for her compassion, her protection of the home, her love of children, and her body is the birthplace of all the world's waters.

BUT WHAT DOES "CHILD-FREE" Miranda find in Yemaya? Given her insatiable interest in male tennis players in shorts, Frederick's of Hollywood, and homemade aphrodisiacs, I doubt that Miranda ever turned to this mermaid mother for lessons in wholesome behavior or enrichment of the womb. More likely she turned to the mermaid for uplifting solace, emboldening comfort. The ultrafeminine, as embodied by Yemaya, would beckon and cradle any young woman lacking a mother-figure to turn to. Miranda, I now think, found comfort in the mermaid's consistent sympathy with those forced to run on legs. With her lessons in love pertaining not so much to carnal pleasure as to maternal tenderness and comfort, sagacious calm, and soothing embrace, this mother of the world's waters, women, and children is an anchor—a woman to call home.

I envision voluminous Miranda stepping up onto a wooden fold-out table, arms spread wide, air conditioner blowing her hair back, Peruvian flutes on the sound system. Right there and then, she could have become a mermaid at the helm of a boat, a siren on a cliff's edge. She could have been like Yemaya: beautiful, stately, and proud with skin the color of unblemished chestnuts and eyes like copper-tinged agates. Land legs caressed by her seven skirts of blue and white, reminding the world of her enchanted half, the lower aquatic extremities scaled in sheaths of pale blue topaz and pure white pearl. Miranda channeled the All Mother if ever there was one—Yemaya sang through her, and all that thick, overtly feminine gardenia perfume made perfect sense.

MIRANDA ON THE TABLE like some old carving at the head of a ship's hull, the quintessence of the primordial goddess figure: the vision came easy. What didn't conjure so well in my mind was the image of my own motherhood (or its voluptuous glory), the idea of a giant belly swelling above crimson scales. The idea of not swimming alone in the sea anymore, of a baby slowing me down—these thoughts stirred a distant feeling of panic, never calm.

When I was young, every story I wrote and every daydream fantasy I lived out in make-believe games and coloring books involved . . .

› *Mermaids swim through the dreams of people—and fish.*

orphanage. Alone in a world that consisted only of winged horses, mermaid tails, and gentle threats of distress that added suspense and adventure to daydreams, but never real or impending harm. The only hint of gore allowed was a bloody cut on my leg (or tail) that required immediate attention from a handsome prince, farmhand, or time-traveler boy. Even as a kid I put aloneness on a pedestal. A streak of independence that manifested itself on the open sea, a desire to be separate in a physical, even supernatural way from everyone else: they were dreams of liberation, and those dreams intensified with age.

As a young woman I thought I would never get married, never settle down but would probably live in a foreign country as an ex-pat and would certainly never strap myself, or my style, down with kids.

There is enough talk of mermaids and the womblike quality of the sea—I felt no need to replicate that aspect of the legend, or the symbolism, with my own body. Just the tail, please.

I'm sure that I even took a long drag off a Gauloise while I was having these thoughts.

But one fire sparks another, while others are slowly extinguished, and Yemaya's influence reached some new corner of my older self. Maybe it was all that fruit and winter light on the beach that added to her appeal, but while living in Seattle I grew to feel Yemaya in the salty breezes, began to sense her presence in the flat faces of the Olympic Mountains. Instead of wanting to fly away—board a plane and land in an unknown city—I started liking my garden, a lot. I began drinking my coffee outdoors every morning, combining the smell of tomato vines with the sound of lapping waves that were only a few blocks away. Earth and ocean: both within reach. Digging my hands into dirt, I wanted to make things grow, and some part of myself—once knotted and tight with restlessness and an impatience to go, to escape the first hint of tedium—eased into a feeling of nurturance that I hadn't experienced before.

Around the time of summer solstice, I planted every variety of tomato I could find: green zebra, heirloom, brandywine, bloody butcher, lemon boy, roma, cherry, early girl, sweet million, garden peach, Siberia, early cascade, jubilee. And I tended to them with the first inklings of a maternal instinct. Wiping their leaves clean of aphids, buying them ladybugs and marigolds, pulling the weeds that blocked their sun, brushing the branching stalks into streamlined steel cages that supported the weight of their fruit and helped them grow big and strong.

The summer passed with the sound of small waves lapping on the shores, nighttime drizzle, and morning-glory days. I'd clip herbs to use in cooking, so much so that my fingers were always fragrant with peppermint and rosemary. The sunflowers were taller than I was, and the pumpkins were starting. I suppose that as a mother gets up in the morning and sleepily walks over to the baby's cradle, or opens her eyes to see her own baby beneath the bed covers next to her, I walked out to the garden when there was still damp mist on the ground to see what changes had occurred overnight, what had been eaten by snails, what had pushed through the loamy soil and fertilizer fish bones while I slept. I hurried out to check on any discernible changes in the plants I'd grown from seeds.

The faintest inklings of possibly wanting to be a mother someday began to flutter in my thoughts, gentle as moth wings. In my mid-twenties, cup of coffee in hand, the day ahead still an unknown—for fleeting moments, I saw visions of my daughter in the garden with me, amorphous as dawn's light and shadow. I barely flinched; there was a mystical quality to it. When I caught sight of her long, blond hair, I wondered which siren I had chosen to name her after. Maybe it was little Ligeia in the garden with me . . . tiny tail under a sundress.

5

Sedna's SEA

*A woman always
has her revenge ready.*

During college, and later in graduate school, I'd taken a keen interest in the anthropology of Arctic peoples. While finishing up my Master's thesis in archaeology, I was working as a curatorial assistant in a museum, and while organizing trays of artifacts and musty yellow papers, I encountered the great sea goddess of the North, carved out of a piece of ivory the size of my palm and wrapped up in cloth.

After I pulled back the layers of pockmarked tissue, I ran my finger along her smooth, scaleless tail, her two long braids, her flattened breasts, her rectangular torso. Her closed eyes were two crescent moons, like fingernails pressed into the roundness of full cheeks. Her name was Sedna.

I was excited. All alone in the museum basement with a new mermaid, I began pulling books off the shelf and reading everything I could find about her—different versions of her story; different ways she has been described, drawn, and dreamt of; different places where her legend reigns and where people are vulnerable to her control of the watery domains. I put an archived cassette into a tape player and listened to one Inuit elder's telling of the Sedna story while the museum's heating vents creaked and groaned in the background like old ships. I discovered sources that explained that the name Sedna is a distortion of the Inuktitut word *sanna*, which means "down there" or "under." When the first missionaries went through the remote Arctic areas and inquired about local gods and goddesses, the people of the North pointed down into the sea, saying *sanna*, and the mistaken name Sedna was thus recorded and has lingered ever since. Across the Arctic regions, however, she is still known by different names: Food Dish, Niviaqsiaq, Talilajuq, Nuliajuk, and more.

Several months later, while we sat on a bench in front of two giant totem poles carved of cedar, with Raven's painted red beak pointing directly at us, an Inuit woman told me her version of the story. As we ate Indian frybread with butter and huckleberry jam and sipped vending-machine coffee, she explained to me in so many words (and I am adding some of my own) that as a young woman, Sedna lived with her mother and father and was spoiled rotten. Sedna had the most luxurious of furs to wear and few responsibilities, all because her father was a great hunter. Their home was stocked with food throughout the year, and Sedna—clothed in her fox-fur wraps and ensconced atop a polar-bear blanket—saw no reason to disrupt her lifestyle of plenty. She had everything she could ever want.

Her parents pleaded with her to marry, but the obstinate Sedna turned each of her suitors away. She laughed in the faces of handsome but poor men, and she lifted her chin, feigning boredom, in the presence of old and wealthy ones. Although both her mother and father were outraged by this irreverent behavior, Sedna would not change it.

Then one day a dashingly handsome youth, a stranger to the village, appeared at the door of her tent. Wearing rich furs and smiling beneath shiny black hair, lovely and slick as polished obsidian, he quickly swept Sedna off her daintily booted feet. He promised her that if she married him, he would provide her with a wealth of furs and every comfort: meat, blankets, few chores, and babies to play with. Sedna was satisfied with the deal—even excited—and she agreed to marry him. Smug in her certainty of imminent wealth, she packed only a small bag of her things, leaving behind the luxuries her parents had given her in expectation of better.

Sedna and the man left for his island the next day. His kayak was a handsome one. The skins were evenly colored, and the oars were crafted with artful expertise: delicate carvings of large-beaked birds swirled around the handles. It was a good start, Sedna thought. The journey to the man's home took all day, but the sea was smooth as glass, and Sedna was able to sleep for much of the trip.

When the bottom of the boat finally slid onto gravelly sand, Sedna's drowsy eyes opened. Eager to spot her new home, she raised herself up from her seat and looked up and down the shore. She saw nothing but barren, windswept cliffs and sharp stone. An unpleasant howling of blustery gales beat her ears, and Sedna shivered under her thick furs.

As a vine of cool fear twisted through her, Sedna turned to her new husband with a nervous smile. Where was the big, comfortable tent? She jumped back with shock as he bent forward and began coughing, then laughing, then cawing like a crow. Feathers burst from his neck, and sharp talons cut through his soft leather boots. His nose changed from flesh to beak, and his once warm brown eyes—charming and affable—turned black and darty. He was no man—he was a bird! When his transformation was complete, he flew in circles around Sedna's head and regurgitated a piece of fish for her that fell on the sand by her feet with a pathetic plop.

Sedna howled into the winds in despair. From now on her only shelter was a tattered fish-skin tent. Since the birdman could not hunt, Sedna was forced to eat raw fish for every meal. Soon her plump cheeks grew sallow, and her shining hair became matted and dull. Cold and homesick, she wept long

Pinky fingers became baby seals; thumbs grew into walruses.

and hard from morning to night. The sound of her weeping was lifted up and carried by southern winds until it reached her father. Worried that something was terribly wrong, he set out to pay his daughter a visit.

When he arrived, he was met at the shore by the thin and unusually scruffy Sedna. She ran to him with arms outstretched and fell at his feet, begging him to take her home. She explained how her husband had deceived them all, and her father, becoming increasingly incensed, kissed the girl's forehead and promised revenge.

After hours of careful searching, he found the birdman asleep in a nest perched high on a rocky overhang. Surrounded by fish bones and gnarled twigs, the birdman breathed easy, his long beak tucked into the black flight feathers of his wing. Outraged by this creature's

cruel mockery of his goodwill, Sedna's father killed him with a single blow of his club to the head. Then he twisted the long, feathered neck until it snapped like a burst of corn kernels dropped in hot oil. The pale ocean below sat still and unchanged, the wind remained steady, and it seemed that the murder had passed unnoticed by the world.

Scurrying back down the cliff, Sedna's father grabbed hold of Sedna's hand and ran for the kayak. Sedna and her father pushed off and pointed the boat home. Unbeknownst to them, however, the birdman's friends had discovered the body of their beaked comrade and were plotting to avenge his death.

In a torrent of black wings that obscured all light from the sky, the birds descended upon the kayak from overhead, flapping their wings until the water was whipped into a wrathful frenzy. Sedna and her father swatted at the biting birds, trying their hardest to slap the nipping beaks back, but waves began to crash over the small kayak. It was almost impossible to keep the boat upright. Terrified of the riotous waters, the whirling suction of riptides, and the slushing of ice (it seemed the whole ocean had been poured into a high-speed blender), Sedna's father grabbed his daughter and threw her over-board in hopes of appeasing the angry avian mob.

The birds only screeched with raucous delight. As they beat their wings in a thunderous racket, the ocean opened up, spewing frothy waves, and ice-water arms grabbed hold of Sedna. She screamed. Screamed for her father to save her and, with a frantic lurch forward, grabbed hold of the kayak's edge.

The boat tipped forward and began to sink. To save himself, Sedna's father reached for his knife and, setting its handle firmly in his palm, raised it high above his head. With a cry of anguish, he brought the knife down towards Sedna's hands. One by one, he cut

‹ *Sedna is revered by the Inuit as mistress of the world's oceans,*
as well as protector of the creatures who live within them.

off each finger at the joint. Sedna's screams mingled with the shrill winds. When the last bone was broken, Sedna fell beneath the ripped surface of the sea.

At first there was only silence. But soon, as each finger drifted though the cold currents, it changed into a beloved creature of the sea. Pinky fingers became baby seals; thumbs grew into walruses. The first whale songs began to fill the ocean with their reverberating melody and bass. Seal laughter rose with the swells; dolphin chatter started in earnest, and pretty courting dances began. And Sedna fell deeper, fell through these layers of jubilant sound. She sank all the way down to the bottom of the seafloor, and when her first toe touched sand, her legs fell together and became a mermaid's tail.

I'VE NEVER LIKED INDIAN frybread very much, but it was worth eating piece after piece to keep the story going, to eat past full so that the woman would continue explaining the origins of Sedna's tail and moods to me. She told her story in slow cadence, her voice rising in excitement only when the sky turned black with the bodies of flying birds and the sea went wild.

Later that day, after leaving the musty-smelling museum basement, I sat by myself on the bench and stared out to the distant mountain-framed water, thinking of how it wasn't only sea kelp that swayed thickly in those Canadian tides, but also Sedna's mermaid hair—as soft and lustrous as the kind you see in shampoo commercials. With all her hair and animals around her, Sedna can control the entirety of the sea—this was the power she gained by the misfortune she suffered—but without fingers, the simplest of tasks became impossible: she can't comb her hair. Her silky strands become tangled, and every day she has to turn her face to the incoming current in an effort to see, to keep her hair from wrapping around her face and covering her eyes.

As in the Melusina legend of European lands, Sedna's tail was both a blessing and a curse. Before the Inuit woman left to go home, she balled up the napkin holding crumbs of her frybread, wiped her mouth, and elaborated on the more personal dimensions of Sedna. We talked about how Sedna is very much alone, unlikely to entertain dreams of little sons and daughters, living, as she does, the lonely life of a queen. As she sits beneath the weight of slow-moving seawater, her swath of sandy floor is still and hushed; her sky is a fractured ceiling of blue northern chill.

She has been rendered in the colors of the melting northern lights—dusky pinks and faint bands of purple. Starlight catches in the curves of her scales, and the winter sun, low and pale, casts her widespread fins in ghostly shadow. She is plump, never bony, and her face is tattooed with black dashes and dots radiating from the corners of her lips and eyes, curving in circles upon her cheeks, and arching above her brows. Her facial tattoos are the mark of womanly beauty and high status.

Although Sedna spends her days in solitude, she is kept company by her sea mammals. The animals that came from her severed fingers stay close. They sleep tangled in her hair: fat seals, whales, and walruses. Swaying in her whorls of dark and tangled tresses, awakening and swimming away from her nest of hair whenever their mermaid commands.

Because it is her commands that feed the people above, the hunters wait by frozen fishing holes with their harpoons ready for the blessings of Sedna. When Sedna is in a benevolent mood, the hunting is plentiful and winter passes without hunger or death. But when she grows moody, when her generosity is abused or taken for granted, revenge arrives by way of empty catch nets and broken harpoon points that thwart all efforts to catch food.

In particular, if a seal is caught, it is because Sedna has released the creature from her supple cage of hair, allowed it to be touched by the harpoon's point. When seal after seal escapes, however, and when the fire has no meat or oil upon it, or when bellies are empty and children cry for want of food, Sedna's foul mood has made itself clear. It rises from the sea like upwelling currents: the result of mistreatment.

For many indigenous peoples of the high North, it is common knowledge that once a seal has been killed it has to be offered a drink of water. Freshwater, not saltwater, poured from the water pouch of the hunter in a gesture of sharing and thanks. Water aids seals on their journey to the spirit world, returning them to the currents of Sedna's

> *The ocean floor is the mermaid's haunt.*

hair. Similarly, after a fish is eaten, every one of its bones must be carried back and delivered to the sea, for the fish is understood never to have *died;* it simply offered itself up as food and will become whole again. The white bones sent back to sea are later reconstituted as new fish, prepared to hook their mouths once more on the fisher's line whenever Sedna asks.

All women are the very sea: treacherous waves, unpredicted rain, frightening depths.

So, with her hair extending for miles and no fingers to hold a comb, water-ruffed by the storm currents and tussles between male seals, Sedna's messed hair becomes her sweet spot. She likes it to be brushed and braided, pulled back from her moon-shaped face in neat lines, plaited and wrapped in strings of soft sinew. Like any mermaid devoted to her locks, Sedna wants her hair to flow smooth as currents, straight and true without snarl. But when her hair is knotted, Sedna becomes frustrated and the animals are stuck in her tresses. People above are starving, and shamans desperate for an end to famine and backed by the prayers of their communities, force their bodies out of their earthly skins and descend through perilous cold and altered consciousness to speak with the great mermaid and, more important, to comb her tangled hair. The lonely queen does receive the occasional visitor.

Although her temper is mercurial and her control over human communities complete, Sedna remains, in part, a woman dependent upon kindness. A mighty mermaid who likes a good head petting:

who can't relate to that? A strong woman who loves the feel of someone smoothing her locks, tucking loose strands into braids, gently brushing a piece of hair behind her ears, and sweeping split ends up and off her neck with the patient stroke of a soft-bristled brush.

I FIND SEDNA REFRESHINGLY moody, verging at times on cranky, even crabby. Her life as a mermaid has never divorced itself from human emotion. The mermaid tail she gained upon falling to the seafloor did not erase the bitterness she felt towards her father and her husband. She never shook her earthly anger. A human woman might stand in her kitchen, furious at a friend or a lover, washing salad leaves and chopping vegetables a little too vigorously while conducting conversations in her head in which she yells her eloquent fury at the person who has upset her. Sedna too must have told off her transgressors in heated fashion over and over again. The things she should have said to that husband of hers and the things she should have done when her father raised the knife! My God, she should have pulled him under the cold sea with her. Internal dialogues of resentment must play in her head tirelessly.

What woman can say she hasn't experienced this? Simmering frustration kept cool by steady countenance, a thought spilling over into a fit? A bout of PMS that leaves you sobbing on the kitchen floor, tears mopped up with a dishrag, only because he forgot to buy the chocolate frozen yogurt you requested when he was at the grocery store. Or maybe you made dinner, and he simply ate it without saying thank you. Or he left the dish for you to put in the dishwasher. I can hear Sedna, *I give and I give and I give*... the quintessential complaint repeated by mermaids and landbound women alike.

Sedna has rage, yet unlike the rest of us, she can thrash icebergs together, make waves, leave every fishing hook bare in malice. We can only... break chairs. Or at least I've done it. Up and over the head in a Sedna-style tantrum, I smashed a chair once in a slightly unreasonable mood. We always told houseguests that the chair simply came that way, that it was part of a set we found at a garage sale. Never mind that it has only three legs.

I see Sedna as a woman confined to the world's most spacious kitchen—the ocean—and involuntarily charged with providing meals for those who reside above. It wouldn't take much to feel taken for granted or underappreciated. This feeling extends to her animals too. She doesn't give their lives away lightly.

Think of those thirsty seals and fish bones. The story of Sedna is intrinsically connected to food—how it is obtained, valued, honored, sustained. How we pay—or should pay—regard and due reverence to the mermaid's lower half. It is a lesson in balance—balance between the tail and the torso, balance between the earth's oceans and the people who eat what's in them. Eating salmon in my own kitchen, I've often thought of the bones. A fish broken apart and shared by many in city apartments who live lives utterly separated. How could the fish ever be put back together—restored to a whole—if its bones can't be collected and returned to the sea? What becomes of the thousands of fish vertebrae in trash cans across the country?

I have heard Sedna's anger when she discovers that some of her animals have been lost to her forever. When the waves near my house have seemed especially restless and choppy, when they pound the shore without soothing or steady rhythm, I have lifted up from dreams and flown from bathwaters into the cool night. Flying along the edges of Canada, over the islands that look like dark blemishes on lapis stone, through rain clouds, and past snowy cedar forests. Like some siren of old, I've got both eagle wings and a mermaid tail. The winds rush past with the sound of blurring lutes. Below me I see flickers of candlelight from seal-oil lamps, truck headlights, and snowmobiles; I hear the barking of dogs. The sound of Sedna's tail pounding the seafloor grows louder as I fly with wings spread towards the icy sea. I dive into a shock of cold so thorough my heart catches and I laugh in its pure brutality—and down I go, mermaid tail pumping.

Sedna is surrounded by floating fish vertebrae and swimming fish; seals sleep in her lap. And I line up with the shamans to take my turn combing her hair. Take my turn comforting and assuring the great mermaid as I make a fishbone braid in her hair that humans do not intend the sloppy harm they sometimes cause; their ungrateful behavior is sometimes just forgetfulness—lack of focus. Really, they don't all mean to disturb the gentle domains of fish and mermaids with their dinner forks.

I SAW SEDNA in the city one night when Laura Nyro sang on a hotel stage. Or at least I saw Sedna convincingly channeled.

Laura Nyro sang blustery, sometimes quiet, sometimes Broadway-show ebullient, songs about love, heartache, moonshine, and rebellion, women and their lives made of lust and loss. The album *Eli and the Thirteenth Confession* is her masterpiece. Her songs reflected street smarts and thick skin, a toughness undercut by this lyrical bell-tone gentleness. Her voice embodied the full spectrum of moods—from spitfire rage to kitten-sweet affection.

When I went to see her perform, I hardly had mermaids on the mind. I was most interested in the fizzy gin and tonic set in front of me and the table conversation, but as the lights dimmed, and tea-light candles were transformed into watery stars, Sedna rose from the sea. Laura was wearing shimmery silver, her wavy dark hair fell past her shoulders, and she was magnificent—an urban siren standing there in a cocktail lounge.

Her voice conjured up the character of the sea itself. It must have carried down city streets, over the heads of tourists and couples in restaurants; it must have gathered itself into blankets of fog and night, smothering the marina in a tinkling start and then completely drowning out the foghorns. Women filled the room—there was a notable absence of men. The occasional male date, perhaps, but it seemed that many had come to the show alone or with women friends. It wasn't the type of concert people talked through. Laura's singing never faded into the background; she commanded rapt attention the whole way through. Like Sedna, she was in complete control.

Akin to Homer's sirens, she sang what her audience most wanted to hear: songs of womanly revenge and of love, of growing up behind her father's back and defying paternal control, and of the affection between two women—both lovers and friends. Her songs rippled out

‹ *Big boats have long pushed through mermaid play—oblivious to enchantments lying just beneath the hull.*

and ran parallel to the lives of the women assembled there. She sang lyrics that could make a man feel like a dog and any woman a hero. You got the feeling that she could lure a lover to her shores and, if disappointed in any way, smash him to smithereens in a full-blooded rage—that, or just make him starve.

Both Laura and Sedna have the quality of women who have been bitten, been through it, street smarts and tough hearts, yet all the while, up here singing, or down there swimming, it's not that they ever become vulnerable; they just give up a part of themselves in temporary trust, be it by comb or microphone. And for that trust, they expect gratefulness and thanks. Fast as a mermaid's tail, that trust can vanish and be replaced by fury, but their womanly grace can also linger, settle like sand before the upwelling current sweeps it up again.

Like women on land, Sedna has some issues that she struggles with. Her reign is supreme but conducted with a slightly bruised ego and a chip or two off the heart. Her trust was abused by the birdman, her faith in human kindness and love destroyed by her father. How many mermaids have found love, been loved, and awakened the next morning to see the ship sailing away with the morning tides? Sometimes the handsome suitor reveals himself to be a shifty black-eyed bird—something to which we can all relate.

But in the end, all women are the very sea: treacherous waves, unpredicted rain, frightening depths that are never altogether knowable. Never eager to please, Sedna is a reminder of our own human storms, a validation of anger and tantrums. Laura's lyrics promised that she could provide or destroy; Sedna shows us how it's done. But we women are also the gentle lapping of sea foam upon sand, the pacifying currents that buoy a person up and let him or her float, belly puffed out, full of good food, and eyes closed to the brightness of the sun.

6

River
OF SEDUCTION

*All rivers do
what they can for the sea.*

THOMAS FULLER, *GNOMOLOGIA*

*H*ome from Seattle to visit family and friends for a long weekend, I got up in the morning and had a cup of coffee with my mom over breakfast, then hopped into the rental car and took myself north and west to the beach in Bolinas. Windows down: it was September, Indian summer in northern California—dry and hot. But even on the hottest days, Bolinas stayed damp and cool from the breezy lagoon air and high eucalyptus canopies.

I parked the car beside the overgrown tennis court, wild with tall-stalked calla lilies and low-lying ferns, passed by loose gatherings of ruffian dogs (who have the same resident status in that little town as people), and walked down the paved ramp, summer-solstice murals painted underfoot, and past the concrete retaining wall towards the public beach.

The water was glittery under the noonday sun, and dozens of surfers, black and shiny in their wetsuits, floated offshore, round as seals. Smoke was in the air, muffled reggae music from radios too, and the place was crowded. There were two directions you could take upon touching foot to sand. The first, if you turned left, led you to the more popular strip of beach, nestled as it was between sea, spit, and cliff. The place to be seen and to find those you wanted to see. It was crawling that day, as packed as an open-air market in June.

To the right, your chances were better of finding a sheltered niche to tuck into. Bleached-out driftwood and long tree branches that had fallen from the eroding sandstone cliffs overhead were strewn throughout the area. You could throw your towel under the silvered bark to find shade for your face or for whatever part of you that started to burn in the glare of sun and sea. Carrying towel, hat, and water, leather sandals dangling from my fingertips, I headed across the cinnamon sand speckled with green-bottle glass and shell. The air rang with the circling sound of clanking iron from a game of horseshoes. I walked along the edge of the water, fixated on its folds and undulations. The wet ground had the texture of an ice-cream sandwich: damp cake, firm and spongy. I walked blindly, not looking up or around until I realized, rather suddenly, that I was staring at the lower arch and slope of a lean woman's back.

My eyes snapped up in surprise; I reoriented myself, taking in the scene before me. Lying flat in the sand, on her belly, was a naked woman the color of sand and old amber. Her hair was like lion fur: haystack hair, tawny and metallic. She was guarded by men and unkempt dogs, who formed a smirking, defensive half-circle around her.

I couldn't help but stare. She was very much a creature of the earth, for even as I unabashedly gawked, I could not always tell where her limbs ended and where sand began. Holding her head in her hand, leaning on an elbow, she returned my stare, smirking ever so slightly

and tossing her head back with a cocky, charismatic arrogance. One of her eyes was blue, the other pale green. Around her neck she wore a strand of shark teeth with a piece of cut jade in the center.

Someone called out her name: "River."

Smoke smarted in my nostrils, and the barking of dogs grew more excited, if not aggressive, as I approached. Sinewy bodies, the smell of cooking meat (well, hot dogs) and cheap incense, and the pounding of a drum circle nearby, punctuated by the cries of gulls, added to my sense that I had stumbled upon some coastal Paleolithic clan gathering. The beach and the people upon it possessed an ancient quality. And this woman, whoever she was, exuded a sensuality that you could nearly smell against the smoke.

My pale Seattle skin felt drab and lifeless—the color of school glue—next to this bronze slip of sculpture lying on the beach. My polka-dot swimsuit began to feel ridiculous. Beside her sandy feet, my leather sandals felt contrived, decorated as they were with blue beads and other mermaidenly accoutrements. The pearl earrings I was wearing felt lame in contrast to her naked shoulders. My suntan lotion with shine was a sham. Within seconds, my mermaid sparkle had drained; the tail had turned back into legs. I could not compete

‹ *Those pretty mermaid tails are what pull men down into deep-sea love and an uncertain fate.*

with the raw sexuality of this River woman. Not that I was trying to compete, exactly. I simply knew that I had met the greater force, had been caught unawares by a rip current, the kind that yanks you out to sea when you're having a pleasant swim. Your only hope of surviving is to let the angry tide have its way, not to fight it or swim against it.

Her hair was like lion fur: haystack hair, tawny and metallic.

You have to swim perpendicular to its pull or it will drag you a mile out from shore.

I walked past the woman like a swimmer extracting herself from the ripping tides: steady and straight, keeping my eyes focused on the way out and away, on the path of least resistance.

Her eyes, however, stared far past me, past the men and past the sand, out to the most distant point on the horizon—out to the remote Farallon Islands, a small M-shaped cluster of stones and seabirds rising from the Pacific like a silhouetted set of fangs.

God dammit, I murmured under my breath, kicking up a spray of sand with my foot.

YELLOW-HAIRED RIVER had both land and sea wrapped around her sandy finger; she had laid herself out where the two meet. Her earthliness made me uncomfortable; it defied the hitherto singular ability of the ocean and its myths to evoke secrets of womanly enchantment. Where was the supernatural tail on such a creature?

It was as if the magnetism of the mermaid had washed up on shore and taken human form, and there it was amplified by brassy self-assurance and modern sex appeal. As I stood speechless on the beach, the mermaid suddenly swam out of my imagination, and for all intents and purposes, stood up and *walked* away on legs.

It was tempting to think that River's seaside nudity was the result of having just stepped out of the tail, that her fins were tucked away somewhere like the selkie's skin, but I didn't think so. My gut said no. She might have oceanic connections, but she was nevertheless pure earth. Looking at her, I knew her to be a woman more likely to dream of lions than fish.

Certainly I was drawn to her power, and more certainly, I wasn't alone. Her circle of admirers sat behind her with simmering reverence: in awe, in lust, in admiration, in bowled-over respect. But one could detect that behind their lust lay fear. Just as sailors have stood on board their boats, jostling each other back and forth, joking about catching a mermaid and random deep-sea love, as soon as the water splashed high, as soon as a wave slapped into another with a resounding clap and swish—they held their collective breath in both eager anticipation and in terror. What sort of woman was about to emerge from the waves? What hell would be unleashed? How could the sea, or she, ever be controlled, approached, impressed?

The men at the beach were glued to River's side—they would never be willing to leave—but they weren't quite comfortable in their staying. The same was true of me. I had heard the mermaids singing, had seen my own tail in its varying shades, but River was a mermaid with new potency. Lying there in the sand, she was a type of beauty that you couldn't shake, the kind of woman who sparked stories—stories of longing, conquest, and make-believe. In that way, she was like a mermaid. In her unearthly stare out to sea, she was like a mermaid. And Homer would have nodded approvingly at her skills of seduction. He couldn't have dreamt of better behind his unseeing eyes.

But she was intimidating in her seductive allure, and mermaids had never been that to me; rather, they were the beckoning alternative. None of us were at ease in the presence of River, but we were fascinated. I stared, and the men stared, and passersby too. All this raises the question: is a woman like this a woman's woman or a pin-up girl? Who crafted this call of seduction?

Before Homer's sirens, merfolk were the utopian expressions of sage counsel and deep-sea knowing: teachers, and hardly objects of desire. But even the sirens, in spite of their lyrical cadence and intent, acquired a sexual reputation after their literary debut in the *Odyssey* that not even they, with their rumored powers of prophecy, could have foreseen. They were transformed from harpy-inspired temptresses to pure harlot.

> ➤ *The svelte embrace of a mermaid*
> *was condemned by the Church as sin.*

I had to wonder if River's foremothers weren't the original sirens of old.

Sirens and mermaids, first sisters of feather and fin and later one and the same, were originally ushered into the sexy seas of sin by the medieval Church. In twelfth-century Europe, belief in the mermaid was never called into question. Illustrated bestiaries from the time depict the mermaid alongside tigers and giant squid, her scales drawn with scientific precision and validated by the authoritative summations of the experts. Her presence in the oceans was thus never a matter of superstition: it was fact. She was a creature of moonlight song, the woman with a fish tail who sat on rocks under stars and sang harmless tunes that rocked babies to sleep and filled quiet harbors with soul and salty spirit. That, or she was a dream to people who lived in the villages and towns—a vision of coastal magic much like the unicorns that gallop through the daydreams of city girls who've never seen a true forest. The mermaid always possessed elements of danger and moodiness, but she had not yet been acquainted with passionate sex and an insatiable hunger for love exceeding all human limits—not until, that is, some leaders of the clergy decided she should be.

The mermaid was chosen to symbolize the treacherous woman, the spoiler of men, and the very literal essence of slithery and snaky evil. Her beauty became more pointed, more expressive of human desire and its trends. Her song was appropriated and reworded. Lip-synching to their own revised tune of seduction's spell, these church leaders interpreted the siren's song to be one of base immorality.

Afloat on the seas of the world and exposed to those relentless as-
saults by the sirens, Odysseus's ship was commandeered as the new
metaphor for the medieval Church. The clergy stuffed homiletic
beeswax into the ears of the laity and bound
their limbs to the Bible with words and pic-   I could not compete
tures. With a heave of determination, the
house of God set itself upon the open sea   with the raw sexuality of
of sin and stationed Odysseus at the helm.
The epic hero represented the ideal saint: this River woman.
confronted with treachery and mortal hin-
drance, assaulted by a thousand seductions, he surmounted them and
stayed true to his course. As would all saved sinners and saints, the
Church declared.

So the mermaid, for better or worse, was corralled into this ocean
of sin and deemed a meretricious temptress with lusty intent; she was
prohibited from the church benches of prayer. So real was their belief
in the fish-tailed seductress that the church actually banned mermaids
from attending service. They were called incorrigible and unworthy
of the sanctified pew.

Although the words sung by the original sirens remain unknown,
"hell-bent" was the scripted message of her new song. Angels were
allowed to fill the sky, gentle and kind in their modest white robes
and their giant wings, but mermaids remained in the soaking wet sea,
symbolic of their newly granted sexual prowess and dark, cavernous,
unreachable depths.

Her reputation thus altered, the mermaid gained—and never quite shook—the water-nymph(omaniac) label. She is the creature who

> . . . found a swimming lad,
> Picked him for her own,
> Pressed her body to his body,
> Laughed; and plunging down
> Forgot in cruel happiness
> That even lovers drown.
>
> W.B. YEATS, "A YOUNG MAN AND OLD"

She is the woman who hunts love like prey, luring her sailor boys into her arms, where they sleep with post-amorous physical exhaustion, and there, spent in the lap of their aquatic lover, she kills them ruthlessly—rarely by accident. Her tail is lethal as a boa constrictor's grip; her lovers might relish the firm embrace when the scales first wrap smoothly around their waists, but as their pelvic bones are crushed to faunal dust and the breath is squeezed out of their chests, their moans of pleasure turn to screams of despair. The mermaid is thus the face put on fear—fear of the ocean's strength and undertow,

‹ *No man has lived to tell the tale of mermaid love.*

its murderous moods and storms, and just as important, it is the fear men feel toward women unbridled in their passions. It is conceivable that fear of womanly strength and sexual ferocity prompted men to call the mermaid a myth—as if women so uninhibited and insatiable could only be creatures of make-believe.

I FELT THE SAME ambivalence about River's riptide of attraction as I did about the issue of mermaid sex and sexuality—about any suggestion of unearthly bliss through carnal delight. Acutely aware of the tide's pull—of the mermaid's acknowledged lust—as I stood on the beach, locked between River's blue and green eyes and the distant M-shaped islands, I wanted to brush the men away from River, wanted to return a mirror and comb to her hands.

It's as if I wanted to swim away from the mermaid's sexy side, take a dive to avoid it.

The mermaid's powers of seduction are her most popular. Both men and women are fascinated by the sexual possibilities of the undersea, which often eclipse the mermaid's other meanings. Oft forgotten are her benevolence and wisdom, in favor of racier qualities. And likely amused by the multiple meanings assigned to her over time by humankind, perhaps the mermaid happily adopted this new role of shameless seducer. Maybe taking the seashell bra off was fun for her. It's certainly been fun for everyone else.

Nevertheless, I couldn't put my finger on my feeling of unease. Was I threatened by this obvious beauty on the beach? Or simply disappointed in the sexual, and hence physically attainable, manifestation of mermaidenly enchantment? In retrospect, I suspect it had more to do with a feeling that sex had won. That sex had consumed the more nuanced mermaid myths, that their complexity had been brushed away to make more room for a blond bombshell. Sculptures and artwork of Sedna are a case in point: over time the Arctic sea goddess has become more and more busty as Western tourists purchase more and more Alaskan souvenirs. Although they may not know the story of her creation, or of her formidable power, many customers do recognize the current cup size (which is, at times, comically huge), and they like it. Today mermaids are fashioned into pin-up girls—any neon mermaid sign illustrates this—yet these caricatures of the mermaid only scratch the surface of River's true and sensual pull.

But can they be ignored?

I went home conflicted and deflated that night, throwing pearl earrings into a box, kicking blue-beaded sandals under the bed, and relinquishing tail-tight jeans for flannel pajama bottoms. I didn't do so because I had encountered humbling beauty; it was sex. Even the suggestion of sex makes the mermaid attainable, and it makes her attainable for men, not women.

Yes, there may be variations of lesbian mermaid love out there, but historically, physical mermaid love has been a gift to, and the scourge of, the male contingent. Her seductive charms have been directed at men; her song has ravished their ears with sweeter promises than her *what if*, which had sustained me through the teenage years. Men could access the mermaid in a way I could not—and wouldn't want to. It was like having your best friend leave you for a man.

Therein lies the frustration of mermaid love: it is precisely her unattainable nature that both thrills and undermines the women who crave a connection to her. And that unattainable quality can vanish. If the medieval Church was right, if every pop culture conjuring of the mermaid is right, the mermaid can be had to some degree. This accessibility is the very thing that colors the fantasies of scuba divers and seafaring poets. And it is what made me feel lost, almost abandoned by the man-eater mermaid. Just like having your girlfriend drop you off at the curb while she struts into a party filled with nothing but adoring men . . . and then you drive home alone.

I EVENTUALLY regained enough interest in my mermaidenly leather sandals to slip them back on and head out to a friend's art opening at a little gallery in San Francisco. Cold glass of pinot grigio fused to my left hand, I meandered through the crowd, and making small talk with the sister of a friend, I noted her necklace—a Venus figurine hanging on a leather cord.

"She's old," I said, lifting it up in my fingers. "Twenty thousand years or so."

> *Human societies have always filled the seas with different kinds of mermaid tales.*

"She's eternal," the woman corrected me, taking a sip of her pink cosmopolitan, and my fingers set the carving back down between her tan clavicles.

We continued our chat, but my thoughts returned to Bolinas Beach, and my attention was directed towards a bowl of black olives next to me: a pod of shiny wet miniature whales all piled together under candlelight. *Eternal.* Personally, I was thinking more along the lines of "timeless." River on the beach, without clothes to denote any time period or fashion, without makeup or hair to suggest anything but natural and untouched, she could have appeared on any of the world's beaches at any time. The unwavering attention paid to her was as much a result of her physical beauty as it was her self-assured sexuality and queenly posture. Although lean as a whip, she evoked the regal presence of the ancient goddess figures of old—round and curvy, bursting with fertility—and, like the mermaid, those timeless womanly symbols have been interpreted in a myriad of ways.

The mermaid was chosen to symbolize the treacherous woman, the spoiler of men.

The Pacific and the Paleolithic share a theme: the complex sexuality of women and how it is understood and interpreted. Archaeologists most commonly ascribe ritualistic significance to the Venus figurines found in ancient Paleolithic sites. The fantastically voluptuous women are thought to have been a centerpiece in fertility rites, perhaps even in mother/earth goddess beliefs and stories. Some suggest that a matriarchy prevailed in those early times and that the out-of-shape female carvings represented some well-fed and plump matriarchs exempted, for whatever reason, from joining the high-activity, hunting-and-gathering lifestyle. Others, however (namely, men), have ventured a guess that the little figurine symbolizes the original—the origin of—pornography (I imagine that this interpretation tells us more about what the archaeologists were thinking than the presumed cave dwellers), that the ample bosom and bottom of this stone effigy were made to satisfy some primordial masculine desire. Here again, one woman's goddess is another man's sex symbol.

Being a true woman's woman, our mermaid finds her earthly ancestry in the footless Venus; and yes, that figure, legs pressed tight together in a little triangle of a tail shape, is suggestive. Both are women of generous proportion and sensuality who deviate from social convention; their explicit femaleness shocks, delights, and mystifies in a manner that appeals to women while, arguably, unnerving men.

Truly, I think it's the glory of womanhood that was and is celebrated—the massively curvy, voluptuous woman of free breast and rolling hip that epitomizes all that is loved and feared most. And the fear is a big part of it. Uncontrollable womanhood, curves that cannot be contained, unapologetic voluptuousness that takes pride in itself—our Venus of the sea, the mermaid ultimately swims free of societal constraint and patriarchal inclination.

As I see it, thousands of years ago, somewhere in a warm cave, with an Ice Age winter covering the land in glacial white, a lanky girl with protruding hipbones, pointed knees, narrow hips, and a hopelessly flat belly would have been pitied. Her friends and relatives would have banded around her, rooting for her like Italian mothers to plump up and eat a second mammoth steak, another bowl of mashed tubers. They would rub her thin limbs with glistening fat and paint red ochre on her thighs. They would laugh and play music. By night's end, the loving hands of mirthful women would change that thin girl into a crimson-tailed mermaid by the light of ancient fires.

MAYBE MERMAIDS, like the rest of us, feel obliged to play the vixen, meet the expectations, cater to male desire. Still, mermaids do exude sensual power. And although the dilemma of the tail and how it works for mutual pleasure goes unresolved, mermaids no doubt enjoy their fun. I won't deny them that.

All of us are attracted to the mermaid's open-sea liberation. We know how freeing it feels to swim topless in the ocean, sea foam pushing up under our arms like a housecat nudging for affection. We feel the wet hair down our backs and the shape of our shoulders in the setting sun. These ephemeral moments of connection to the air, the sea, the light, are the kind you experience when you're alone or in the company of women friends, not when your boyfriend is sitting behind you on the beach, drinking a beer and waiting for your return. They require a sense of the infinite.

As does the mermaid.

FLYING BACK HOME to Seattle, I was sitting in a window seat, face pressed to the glass, as our plane did a wide loop past the coast. Down below I could see the familiar shoreline, the bluffs, beaches, and lagoon. The Farallon Islands stood off at a distance, floating in salmon-colored waters as the sun set in the West. The islands seemed hard to get to, far away and mysterious, formidable and inhabited only by large colonies of seabirds. I liked to think that sheer cliffs made it impossible for any boat to push up on shore, that the place remained remote and unknown—that it couldn't be opened or ever fully known except by the brave few.

When we landed, I waded through the baggage claim to get my luggage and stood waiting for my ride home. It was late, but I bought a cup of coffee anyway. Beneath fluorescent lights and surrounded by crowds, circulating baggage, and excited reunions, I looked down at my white paper cup, and a siren of old stared back at me. The Starbucks logo places her center stage, and frankly she seemed uninspired. Tail spread in two, flaunting her sexuality and singing a song of commercial seduction, the mermaid had been hooked and branded. As I stepped outside to the curb, I could feel the coastal salt in the air. Nevertheless, the wine-dark sea suddenly tasted of little more than vanilla latte.

Rusalki REVELATIONS

And I—
     submerged in water,
          suspended in light,
in this half world
          of seeming—
I dissolve
          like salt
turn
          return
a creature of the sea.

KAREN YELENA OLSEN, "MERMAID"

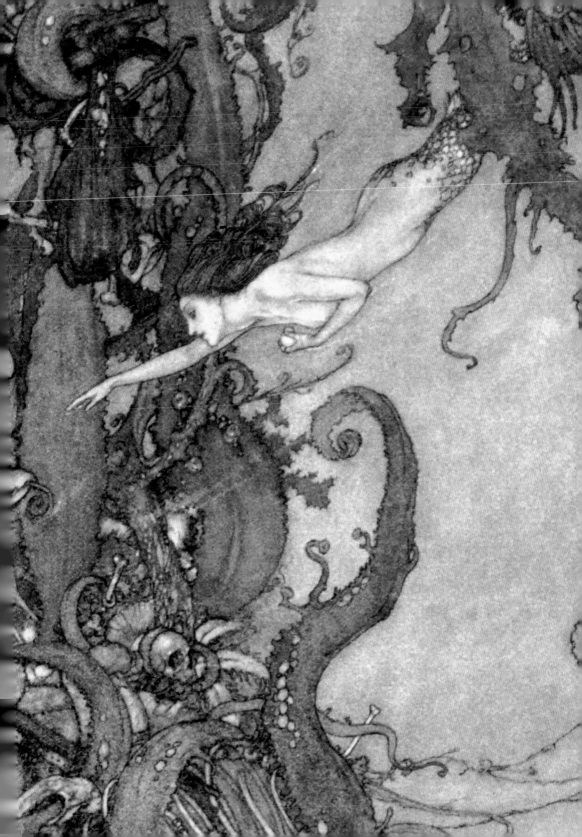

Very few mermaid marriages work out. Sedna encountered only hardship, hunger, and deceit in her attempt at matrimony; that husband of hers turned rancid with a beak. Melusina exchanged vows with the first eligible man she came upon in the woods, only to bear monster children and have her trust betrayed. Selkies endure human marriage but can't wait to bail. And while human grooms might marry mermaids for love, they soon discover, as the pretty tails pull them under, that the wedding ceremony takes place on the ocean floor. Whether or not they remain alive for the festive event is a matter unsolved. Nothing if not happy on their own, most mermaids eschew the whole monogamy thing altogether. It would cramp the freedom they live by.

So I was getting married.

After twenty-seven years of questing for the mermaid, taking my cue from her free-floating lifestyle, her sea smarts and inhibition, I was drifting off course. I was tossing an anchor to the sandy floor and deciding to stay put, or at least to swim alongside another. But the inspiration to get hitched did start with swimming, and that made it seem all right.

We were working in Israel for a summer, on an archaeological excavation south of Haifa. Technically, we first met in the Dead Sea, but that's not the right place for a love to begin, so I prefer to remember our more significant meeting, in the Red Sea, a place much more suited to the fires of romance. About two hundred feet from the shoreline was a reef and beyond that a sheer drop-off into bands of turquoise depth: light turquoise, bright, dark, then navy. And now the confession that should have surfaced earlier: I am afraid of deep water.

Perhaps it was all the near-drowning as a child—the strong undertow, the mermaid determination that made me run into freezing Pacific waves where I'd get water up my nose and stumble out coughing—that stirred up some long-lasting fear, but whatever the case, swimming in extremely deep water is about as frightening to me as flying. No way to touch bottom, nothing to grab hold of—water is strong.

We were standing on the reef with snorkeling gear. The snorkeling off the Egyptian coast of the Sinai Peninsula is some of the best in the world. How I wanted to dive in! But each time I peeked under the water's surface, I got dizzy with the bottomless depth and pulled my head up out of water, hair streaming and heart full of fear. I was pacing like a dog about to be sick when Dan swam up behind me and grabbed me by the waist, and suddenly we pushed off the reef together and dove down. Encircling my hips, his arms felt as good to me as the snug start of a tail.

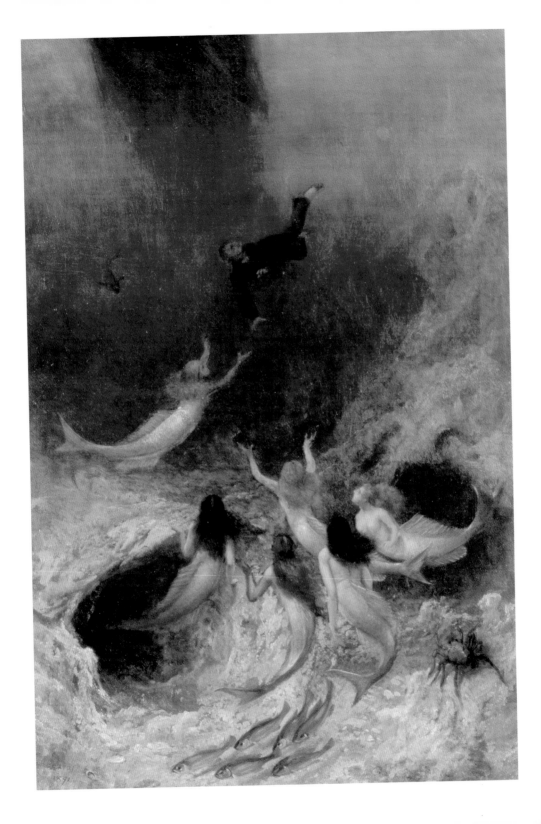

The water was warm, bathtub warm, and this eased my trepidation. In this sea, unlike the ocean where I grew up, hypothermia wasn't chattering down my neck, and in place of pulling undertow was water like silk. When I opened my eyes underwater, it was the fish that took my breath away; the crystal castles, mother-of-pearl shells, sunken pirate treasure, and coral gardens. Thousands of fish as bright as jungle parrots swam through our legs and breezed by my waist, and the best part is that every fish swimming down there was *smiling*. I think that deep down I've wanted to write a book just so I could tell the world that: that fish really do smile in this adorable, goofy way when they are not dead and lying on ice.

I figured that if we could make such a stunning dive on our first weekend together, we could handle whatever storms came our way. And our swim was just . . . lovely. Feeling like a deep-sea mermaid, in tune with other ocean creatures, sharing it with someone else.

Water was a big part of our first summer together. Another day I was playing in the waves, letting them catch me, pull me backwards, then pummel me forward. I threw my body into an especially high swell, which rolled me right into Dan's arms. I didn't know he was there; he had become a part of the singsong, swaying waves. In that

‹ *A chancy dive into the sea is*
rewarded by beauties not known before.

moment there was no transition between saltwater embrace and human. I thought I might just go ahead and marry the ocean in him one day.

So it was in late September, three years later, that I sat in a bathtub alone, my wedding dress hanging on the door. I was washing my hair, dunking it back into water I had made fragrant with Minnesota honey and California cream, letting it rock from side to side, feeling that good mermaid hair feeling. I was conjuring up my favorite mermaids of all: best for last, the rusalki.

No rusalka married and lived happily ever after. Rusalki are the matrimonial rebels of the Slavic regions, the women who flout every expectation. On my wedding day, I wasn't hoping to become one, but I did want them to be an intrinsic part of my day. It wasn't about mermaid emulation—it was about embracing an important mermaid lesson.

RUSALKI ARE THE mermaid cowgirls: wily, rowdy, answering to no one. They're most famous for their pendulous breasts—so large they can be tossed over their shoulders—and for their love of gauzy white dresses. Their eyes shine with green fire, and their unruly,

> *No one ever claimed that mermaids don't enjoy a good time.*

moss-colored hair is always worn down and undone. They keep it wet and tangled, voluptuously long and damp, always free. Rumor has it that their skin must remain perpetually moist for them to stay alive; if ever their skin or their hair dries out, they die.

I leaned my head back into the bathwater.

The rusalka's life is free of any responsibility beyond accepting the annual offerings of devoted believers, and most of her days are spent in rambunctious frolicking, laughing and singing in fields and forests with her sister rusalki. When without the tail, she climbs trees and hides in branches above lakes or rivers, which reflect her mischievous face and long locks. She waits for a man to walk by and become smitten with the ravishing, green-haired girl he sees in the water. Then she jumps on his back, wraps him in her hair, and drags him underwater, tickling him all the while. Agonizing delight turns lethal: the rusalka *tickles* her victim to death.

That, or she sometimes just laughs. Laughs and laughs and laughs, spinning circles and dancing in manic glee till her victim simply falls down with the pleasure and pain of it all. There are men who have managed to escape the rusalka, but once a man sets eyes upon her, his eyes glaze over with a faint blue film and his once cheerful disposition grows morose and distracted. The black pupils of seeing drown in a murky sea of sky blue.

When rusalki sisters are not out to cause mischief or tempt passersby with carnal pleasures and moon-bright skin, they sit together on the edges of riverbanks clapping, yelling, and singing under Slavic stars like teenage girls at camp. Fanning sprays of pond water with the tips of their tails, these mermaids are the reincarnated spirits of young women who died badly before their time. Brokenhearted by unrequited love, murdered by lovers, hanged at the galley as punishment for pregnancy out of wedlock—these were some of the causes of their demise and subsequent transformation. In some cases they are believed to be the souls of unbaptized or stillborn babies; in others, rusalki are defined as the ghosts of drowned women, women who walked themselves to the town's bridge and, like Virginia Woolf with pockets full of rocks, jumped over the side and sank to the cobblestone bottom.

No rusalka married and lived happily ever after.

The rusalka's soaking wet, untamed hair is important and symbolic of things beyond herself. In parts of rural Russia, a woman's hairstyle is symbolic of her status in society and her stage of life. A young girl wears a single braid down her back decorated with ribbons, feathers, and brightly colored beads. Later, as a married woman, she is required to wear her hair in two braids, both of which are wrapped and hidden beneath a headdress. The rusalka defies both traditions.

When a marriage match is made for a girl, the men—the future groom, the girl's father, and the matchmaker—pray together, light candles, and drink wine while the girl's hair is ceremoniously covered with a kerchief. She sits alone with that swatch of linen on her head, a light hand of new ownership perched upon her scalp. Amid

the deep-voiced mumblings and frequent handshakes, the bride-to-be overhears the trajectory of her life discussed and mapped without her. *Yes, she will move away; yes, she will have many children; yes, she is a very hard worker and* (laughter) *a fine dancer too.*

As her wedding day draws near, her hair is repeatedly lathered with honey and butter. Her girlfriends, even her brothers, wash and comb the girl's hair until it is lustrous and moisturized, sleek with sweet saturation. They braid it and then wash it, braid it and then wash it once more. And if anyone squeezes the bride's locks with both hands, honey pours out. This cycle of grooming the bride's hair lasts several days. When the day of the wedding arrives, the bride's girlfriends drink her bathwater in the hope that they too may be so fortunate as to find husbands.

En route to the ceremony, the bride's hair, for the first and last time in her public life, is let loose. Channeling the heterodox rusalka, the bride shines in a moment of glossy-haired radiance. Over her shoulders fall thick waves of oiled tresses: plaited hair released from bands, rolling with crimped bumps of highlight and luster. In that short ride from doorstep to church, the bride enters a liminal state, one where she is neither young maiden nor married wife. She simply is, and is completely herself: her parents have let her go, and her husband has yet to claim her. Fifteen minutes of escorted liberation. Anyone watching this nuptial procession roll by would surely feel compelled to bow or kneel, to run and embrace this veritable mermaid in a wedding dress, with the long hair.

Channeling the rusalka is not necessarily intended as an act of reverence or respect, however. Not on behalf of all. Rather, she is symbolically called upon by clergy during the matrimonial mass only long enough to demonstrate that within the Church she may be conquered. Mermaids and churches have always had an uneasy relationship.

‹ *Rusalki are river maids, famous for their mischievous nature and for tickling men to death.*

The bride's disheveled hair is deliberately allowed to hang wild and free only so that it may captured and restrained. In the church, the bride is summoned to the altar, and standing before her husband-to-be, her hair is covered, braided, and hidden for good. In the relinquishing of her unbound locks, the bride hands over her freedom and autonomy, for life. One can almost hear the water-dwelling rusalka wail with outrage. Like Homer's sirens, their voices mount dangerously, and the harm they can cause, and likely will, increases.

Mermaids are the tremendous creatures of "what if."

A husband waiting in eager anticipation for his long-haired wife to come into bed surely hears some part of the sirens' seductive song. Watching his young wife brush through that hip-length hair (hair saved for his eyes alone), many a man must lean back on downy pillows and envision the sirens of old. The unbound locks framing a wife's face and flowing down her back summon the presence of the rusalka right there in the bedroom, sitting demurely on a quilted couch, within reach and kept. And like a thunderstorm outside my bathroom windows, I hear the rusalki screaming, howling, *No! No! No!* No woman is to be owned, possessed by another. No woman should acquiesce to the shackles of patriarchal society. No man should swim in her hair whenever he pleases, no woman should be forced to live without long white dresses and moonlit parties. Why do you think the rusalka jumped?

Those drowned women sank in their wedding gowns.

Brides with hair wild, free and moist, all buttery and smelling sweetly of honey, jumped carriage and left their grooms-to-be waiting, indefinitely, at the altar. Headdress and braid wraps left on the street, fathers and brothers dumbfounded at the church's door, the girl in the wedding dress ran with her loose hair flying behind her, past cottages and horses, children and carts, until she reached the swift-moving river. Jumping then, hair in a vertical sheet above her head—a wind-whipped banner of freedom spread high as a flag—she plunged into the tumultuous currents knowing that death was close, but mermaidenry was closer. The gauzy dress she awoke to find herself in, the faint spirit of the heavy white gown her sisters buttoned her into.

Not all souls of drowned women become enchanted water spirits—only the souls of women who wished to drown. Women who wished to dance merrily in grassy fields in the company of sisters, wished to shrug off the suffocation of marriage, of motherhood, and of obedient servitude. Perched on a great tree bough, or swimming in a lake, always laughing high above the heads of men, these rusalki forsook the constriction of the headdress for the freedom they coveted.

I had no desire to throw on a bathrobe and run to the ocean, which was only down the street, and jump into crashing waves. But I was checking in with myself. What was I giving up in marriage, and what was I gaining? Would part of the rusalka carry on in me, or would she wither at the altar?

Rusalki sum up what mermaids mean to me and, I believe, what they have meant to people since time immemorial, since a fish-tailed god explained the basics to humankind. Mermaids are the blithe spirits of women untamed, they are the part of all women—enchantresses, mothers, goddesses, girls—who swim always in the ocean, women who are willing to play and to love but who keep themselves ever so slightly unattainable. They are women who have secrets. They are women who can tap into the glamour and mystery of the sea while they walk on city streets. The selkie might remain in a loveless marriage, a union she finds less than satisfying, but she is forever aware of her way out. Never losing sight of the freedom that was once rightfully hers, she does not abandon it; she simply waits for it to return. And it does.

Mermaids are the tremendous creatures of *what if.* They never recede into mere fairy tale, never sink beneath the shores of the imagination, because every woman can find some part of herself within the fish-tailed woman: dazzling beauty, reckless flirt, quiet mother, strong Sedna.

I was swimming in the Caribbean to celebrate my twenty-first birthday. Not in the deep water that I have that healthy respect for, but in the big waves that carry you up for a second and then bring

> *Like the sea, mermaidenry*
> *inspires wistful longing.*

you back down to sugar sand in the next. It was sunset, and the sea foam was sloshing around my shoulders, pulling through my hair. I remembered how the Little Mermaid's grandmother explained that mermaids never die, that after three hundred years they become foam on the sea. And there, somersaulting in the ocean's arms, I was awash in the champagne of ancestral sea sirens: a lacy caress of all the mermaids that have ever been.

The world's love affair with the mermaid was born there, in sea foam. Women will always feel a certain beauty in the sea, a sense of belonging. It is as though all the souls of women before them are kept there, and swimming through them delivers a heightened sense of power, a connection to something larger than landlocked life. The salty hands of a thousand women wrapped around you.

The sealskin might stay folded in the drawer, but the ocean would still flow through my blood.

It's easy to feel the tail when your legs undulate with natural ease in currents, but even standing in jeans on a crowded city street, you can be attuned to the tail. My wedding dress, when I put it on, would cover my legs. It would wrap tight around my hips and fan out at the bottom, a white silk tail gliding down the aisle as I held on to my father's arm. The lesson of the rusalki is that human life need not be abandoned to partake in the freedoms of mermaidenry. For what did they die for? Only the chance to live their lives as they wanted to live them. To wear their hair as they liked, to shrug off societal expectations that threatened to drain the very life out of them. Women today don't live without hardship, not in the least bit, but the mermaid offers a form of solace, if not complete inspiration. Things the rusalka died wanting—freedom to live her life as she liked, freedom to wear her hair as she liked, freedom to beat out her own path—are things that many women enjoy today without threat of repression.

Much of the mermaid myth—and the word *myth* perhaps is a misnomer—has been told by men, men who have written her power away through skepticism and even hostile disbelief. Natural history has discredited the mermaid; science has netted her, dissected her, and labeled her on a shelf. Assuming that mermaids are creatures of the sea alone makes her too simple; for in truth, it is only half the story, the half that worries too much about the improbability of the fish-scaled bottom.

What about the woman on top?

I dried off and put on my wedding dress. My girlfriends sat with me, and we drank champagne to calm our nerves. Mitten was there, and she too had been ringed. The white glitter on her finger was a sign to all that she had voluntarily stepped out of her sealskin somewhere on those wind-ruffed English beaches. The back of my dress got wet from my hair that I wouldn't brush up. The rubber bands and hair spray, the flowers to weave into the braids—they all sat untouched on the bathroom counter. I could feel the water trickling down my back and the form-fitting silk of my dress expand with the moisture. *If a rusalka ever dries out, she will perish.*

The photographer came and we took pictures. The phone was ringing from guests on cell phones wondering where we were and what was taking so long. A car was honking out front. But I kept my hair down, wanting to prolong this mermaid moment.

My mother grew impatient, and I knew the string quartet was tuning its instruments by now. Walking into the bathroom, still dense with bathtub steam, I threw red rose petals into the wet tub—a marker that my crimson scales were still with me and would still be there when we returned to the cottage that night. I grabbed the brush and pulled my own hair back. It was my decision to marry, to braid my hair, to share my life and become a wife, maybe even a mother.

The sealskin might stay folded in the drawer, but the ocean would still flow through my blood; even wedded, I would remain as inspired by the sea enchantress as ever. Some looping braids clipped to the nape of my neck, two garden roses pinned above. My hair was captured and would later be released. That's the best I could ask for: both worlds—land and sea. It's never been hard to navigate both.

Notes

Throughout this book, I've taken the liberty of expanding the stories a little, adding detail as I imagine it and fleshing out the proverbial tale a bit. References noted here informed my understanding of the traditional stories and legends, as well as contemporary viewpoints of mermaidenly interpretation.

The book's epigraph, "The Mermaid," by Tatiana Shcherbina, was published by University of Michigan Press in 1992 and is reprinted by permission.

INTRODUCTION

Ella E. Clark's *Indian Legends of the Pacific Northwest* (1953) provided the point of departure for my discussion on early Native legends about how the first people arrived in North America. I refer to "various collections" because a good deal of oral tradition, as well as current scholarly work, suggests that the first people to cross over into North America did so by boat. It's a lively debate among archaeologists (to put it cheerfully), and it challenges conventional theories on how the first people arrived and, more important, when. The postulated use of watercraft has the potential to push the first arrival period back tens of thousands of years. Native peoples have long explained this to be the case, and today's scientific community is finally catching up.

Discussion of Oannes and Damkina was informed by the wonderful *Sea Enchantress: The Tale of the Mermaid and Her Kin* (1965) by Gwen Benwell and Arthur Waugh, a must-have reference book for all mermaid lovers.

CHAPTER 1

Professor Emeritus D.L. Ashliman, University of Pittsburgh, has conducted extensive research into the folklore of Melusina. He has compiled an online library of folklore, folktales, fairy tales, and mythology that provided the framework for part of this chapter.

The quote by Marcel Proust is excerpted from *Les Plaisirs et les Jours* (1896).

CHAPTER 2

Excerpts from the *Odyssey* are taken from Robert Fagles's 1996 translation.

The late Alan Dundes's *Bloody Mary in the Mirror: Essays in Psychoanalytic Folkloristics* (2002) and Meri Lao's *Sirens: Symbols of Seduction* (1998) both informed this chapter's overview of siren-to-mermaid nomenclature.

What if . . . is from Tori Amos's "Silent All These Years" track on the *Little Earthquakes* album, released in 1991. The lyrics are under copyright in the name of M. Ellen Amos. Permission to reprint the lyrics was generously granted by Sword and Stone Publishing, Inc.

Passages are from "The Professor and the Siren" (1957) in Giuseppe Tomasi di Lampedusa's book *The Siren*, published by Harvill Secker © 1995 by Random House U.K.

CHAPTER 3

The epigraph for this chapter is an excerpt from the poem "The Dancing Seal" by Wilfred Wilson Gibson, found in his book *I Heard a Sailor* published in 1925 by Macmillan and Co.

Selkie sources include Martin Puhvel's article "The Seal in the Folklore of Northern Europe," published in the journal *Folkore* 74 (1963), Sigurd Towrie's comprehensive "Orkneyjar: The Heritage of the Orkney Islands" Web site, *Scandinavian Folk Belief and Legend* (1988) edited by Reimund Kvideland and Henning K. Sehmsdorf, and the work of the aforementioned Professor D.L. Ashliman. John Sayles's film *The Secret of Roan Inish* (1994) is a beauty to watch and also influenced this chapter.

David Thomson's exquisite little book, *The People of the Sea: A Journey in Search of the Seal Legend* (1954 copyright held by Counterpoint Press) is highly recommended reading for all selkie fans. As Thomson notes in his section "The Music of the Seals," the old ballad "The Great Selkie o' Suleskerry" was first written down in 1938 by Dr. Otto Anderson, who heard it sung by a man on the island of Flotto, Orkney. Joan Baez later recorded this traditional song.

Let's go down to the Mermaid Café... is from Joni Mitchell's "Carey" on her masterpiece album *Blue*. Words and music by Joni Mitchell © 1971 Joni Mitchell Publishing Corp. All rights reserved.

Mitten is real and currently lives in San Francisco's Mission District.

CHAPTER 4

Information on Yemaya and the Santeria religion was derived largely from Joseph M. Murphy's *Santeria: African Spirits in America*, Miguel A. De La Torre's *Santeria: The Beliefs and Rituals of a Growing Religion in America* (2004), and a range of online resources with university affiliations.

CHAPTER 5

As noted in this chapter, there are several versions of the traditional Sedna story. Over the years, I have heard so many versions that it is difficult to cite any one source. Many Native legends and stories are not written down, and the stories that have shaped my telling of Sedna's tale were shared with me in conversation, not text. Interested readers will find reference to Sedna in just about any collection of Inuit tradition, art, legends, and/or folklore. In addition, Rachel Attituq Qitsualik authored an informative and interesting discussion of the Sedna story in a four-part series published in *Nunatsiaq News* (1999).

With regard to Sedna's ever-growing bosom and her physical transformation over time and through artwork, Professor Nelson Graburn of the University of California at Berkeley, Department of

Anthropology, gave an especially insightful talk on this subject that I was able to attend. His work on tourism and the art of the Arctic is authoritative.

CHAPTER 6

The discovery of the Venus of Willendorf at a Paleolithic site near Willendorf, Austria, in 1908 launched a thousand interpretations of what her oversized female figure symbolized approximately 24,000 years ago (not to mention what it means today). Very little is known about the figurine's creation or its cultural significance, though it is commonly thought to have been used in fertility rituals. Similar carvings are found throughout Europe; all are generally referred to as Venus figurines.

CHAPTER 7

The epigraph for this chapter is an excerpt from Karen Yelena Olsen's poem "Mermaid." Copyright 1999 by Karen Yelena Olsen. Used by permission of the poet.

The primary reference for this discussion on the rusalki is Philippa Rappoport's excellent article, "If It Dries Out, It's No Good: Women, Hair and Rusalki Beliefs." This article was published in the Slavic and East European Folklore Association *SEEFA Journal* (1999). Other sources include "The Man Who Danced with the Rusalky" from *The Magic Egg and Other Tales from Ukraine* (1997) by Barbara J. Suwyn, and Felix J. Oinas's *Essays on Russian Folklore and Mythology* (1985).

Acknowledgments

No sustained creative effort spares friends and family from those shifting moods the blank page inspires. My loving thanks to Dan for watching me all but channel the tempestuous Sedna at times. This book would not exist without him. I also wish to thank my parents, Kathy and Scott, especially my mother, whom I have always considered to be a true writer within. My brothers, Kevin and Tim(my), are my creative lifeblood and I love them. Thanks also to my grandmother Lorraine Shea, my favorite storyteller.

Without Ann and Jay Jost, this manuscript would have been handwritten on binder paper—their support means the world to me. In addition, Rob Sanders and Nancy Flight at Greystone Books were willing to take a dive into unknown literary waters with me; for that, I will always be appreciative. Special thanks go to Nancy for her wonderful job editing this book.

There are friends who have inspired bits and pieces of this story: Heather Hopp, Erisa Coppernoll, Caroline Lizarraga, Emily Cook, Mikiala White, LeeAnn Barnes, Shanda Hunt, Amanda Grace, Erica Silbersher, and Scout, my mer-girl.

Last, I wish to thank my predecessors of mermaid and selkie lore: the taletellers of old, the believers, and the women who have stood on stormy beaches, inspired by the pounding of waves, surely feeling what I feel today. This connection means everything.

Illustration Credits

Index